I0023142

American Art Association

Vassili Verestchagin Collection

American Art Association

Vassili Verestchagin Collection

ISBN/EAN: 9783744650991

Printed in Europe, USA, Canada, Australia, Japan

Cover: Foto ©Thomas Meinert / pixelio.de

More available books at **www.hansebooks.com**

AMERICAN ART GALLERIES

ILLUSTRATED DESCRIPTIVE CATALOGUE

OF THE

VASSILI VERESTCHAGIN

COLLECTION

ON EXHIBITION PREVIOUSLY TO BEING SOLD
BY AUCTION, WITHOUT RESERVE

DATES OF SALE

NOVEMBER 17TH AND FOLLOWING DAYS

AT 8 AND 2.30 O'CLOCK, P.M.

THOS. E. KIRBY, AUCTIONEER

AMERICAN ART ASSOCIATION, MANAGERS
NEW YORK
1891

BULGARIAN.   SERBIAN WOMAN.   ROUMANIAN.

I trust that men will love me ; for my art
Speaks to the nobler feelings of the heart,
Renders good service by the charm of truth,
And for the vanquished ever pleads for ruth.

(Adapted from PUSHKIN.)

THE historical details, some of which directly, others indirectly, concern my studies and pictures of Palestine—that interesting land for every Christian—are founded chiefly on traditions so well preserved among the people of the East.

My own researches excepted, I have availed myself of the Gospels and old books, as well as of some modern compilations, such as Murray's *Syria and Palestine*, Cook's *Handbook for Palestine and Syria*, Isambert's *Orient*, Brother Lievin's *Terra Sainte*, etc. Some of the studies are very small, my intention having been to repaint them a larger size. Some are unfinished, owing to the suspicion of the Turks that I was drawing plans of the "Promised Land."

My impressions of travel in India formed themselves into a series of large pictures, in which I conceived the idea of representing the history of the conquest of a large Asiatic country by a handful of brave and enterprising Europeans. The first picture, commenced on a large canvas, was intended to portray the English Ambassadors in the presence of the Great Mogul in his celebrated audience hall at Agra. The next pictures were to represent different prominent events of Indian history, finishing with the triumphant entry of the Prince of Wales into Delhi, symbolical of the definitive conquest of the country. This last scene, which I witnessed in 1875, is the only one of the series completed, because the outbreak of the Russo-Turkish war at that time took me away from my studio to the battle-fields.

*　　　*　　　*　　　*　　　*

Observing life through all my various travels, I have been particularly struck by the fact that even in our time people kill one another everywhere under all possible pretexts, and by every possible means. Wholesale murder is still called *war*, while killing individuals is called *execution*. Everywhere the same worship of brute strength, the same inconsistency ; on the one hand men slaying their fellows by the million for an idea often impracticable, are elevated to a high pedestal of public admiration : on the other, men who kill individuals for the sake of a crust of bread, are mercilessly and promptly exterminated—and this even in Christian countries, in the name of Him whose teaching was founded on peace and love. These facts, observed on many occasions, made a strong impression on my mind, and after having carefully thought the matter over, I painted several pictures of wars and executions. These subjects I have treated in a fashion far from sentimental, for having myself killed many a poor fellow-creature in different wars, I have not the right to be sentimental. But the sight of heaps of human beings slaughtered, shot, beheaded, hanged

V. VERESTCHAGIN'S STUDIO.

· uᵤder my eyes in all that region extending from the frontiei of China to Bulgaria, has not failed to impress itself vividly on the imaginative side of my art.

And although the wars of the present time have changed their former character of God's judgments upon man, nevertheless, by the enormous ·energy and excitement they create, by the great mental and material exertion they call forth, they are a phenomenon interesting to all students of human civilization. My intention was to examine war in its different aspects, and transmit these faithfully. Facts laid upon canvas without embellishment must speak eloquently for themselves.

*   *   *   *   *

Next to the pictures where people are slain by the hundreds of thousands, there are some not uninteresting scenes of individual killing in the continual strife waged by the state against persons called criminals.

In olden and more barbarous times the aim of an execu- · tion was to torture the criminal by killing him as slowly as possible ; now, on the contrary, the aim is to kill him as speedily as possible and shorten his sufferings. From this point of view the English method of *blowing from guns* (94, *g*), practiced in India, is the most humane—this mode of execution is sure, quick, and therefore nearly painless ; at the same time the moral impression produced by it is very great, and well suited to the spirit of contemporary law.

The next most humane method of execution is by *hanging*, an old expedient, very much resorted to in Russia in modern times (94, *h*). This method is inferior to the former, because death is more lingering and cruel. But still it is an advance upon the very old system of crucifixion much practised by the Romans (94, *f*). By this latter the man who violated the law was nailed to the wood of the cross, and hung there often many days, during which ·ime his sufferings must have been terrible.

CATALOGUE.

FIRST NIGHT'S SALE,

Tuesday, November 17th, beginning at 8 o'clock
promptly.

*** Measurements are given in inches; the first figures
indicating the height of the canvas.*

---

1. The Tomb of Abraham.
7 × 4½

This tomb lies in Hebron, one of the oldest cities in the
world. Here Abraham was visited by the three travelers
who predicted the birth of Isaac and the destruction of
Sodom and Gomorrah. Besides Sarah and Abraham himself, Isaac, his wife Rebecca, and many other patriarchs, are
buried here. Hither, too, was brought from Egypt the
embalmed body of Jacob, and it is probable that the
mummy is still in a state of good preservation.

This place, containing undoubtedly the true tombs, has

I. THE TOMB OF ABRAHAM.

been held in great veneration from the earliest time by Jews, Mohammedans, and Christians. The upper part has minarets of later Mohammedan workmanship ; it is only below, where the stones are blackened by age, that the wall of David's time begins. The sketch is taken from the roof of a neighboring house behind ; it was impossible to make a more finished picture as the population is most fanatical, and looks upon all attempts at sketching as a profanation of the holy site. They threw stones at us. Christians are very seldom allowed to enter the mosque (the Prince of Wales was allowed to enter in 1862), and in the Grotto itself no Christian traveller has ever been admitted. The Rabbi Benjamin, who lived in the twelfth century, affirms that he saw the real graves of the patriarchs.

2. Bethel.
4¼ x 6¼

Interesting remains of a cistern, probably of Jewish origin. On the heights, where are some Roman ruins, Abraham fed his flocks, and here he divided them with his nephew Lot. Here Jacob slept, as the Arabs sleep now, with a stone for his pillow, and saw in a dream a ladder reaching to heaven, with angels ascending and descending. Here he raised an altar on the place where God spoke to him, and on this spot was afterwards raised a temple, and a city built, which, according to Jewish tradition, was so large that when the Romans broke in on one side, feasts and weddings were being celebrated in perfect tranquillity on the other (?). At the present day there is nothing but a miserable village near the cistern.

3. The Dead Sea.
9 x 13

View from the foot of Mount Quarantania, in a grotto of which, according to the tradition, Christ fasted and prayed forty days.

Only the northern part of the Dead Sea is seen from here,

not the southern part, where, according to another tradition, Sodom and Gomorrah were situated. We are not told how these two cities perished ; but it may be supposed that the bitumen, of which there are quantities in the neighborhood, took fire spontaneously, and as the houses, like the celebrated tower of Babel, were probably built of the same inflammable material, the two places would in one minute have been transformed into an immense brazier. A volcanic eruption, ordinarily followed by earthquakes, would probably have made the catastrophe still more complete and terrible. Vegetation was destroyed, and the waters of the lake subsided. These are so highly impregnated with salt (more than 30 per cent.) as to keep men's bodies afloat, and no fish or living creature can exist in them. Ducks and other aquatic birds may be seen resting on the surface for awhile, but not for long ; and the shores and surrounding country are wilder and more desolate than the salt lakes in Western Tibet and the region near Ladak.

Behind the Dead Sea, as shown on the study, are the Moabite mountains ; on the right, some distance off, is the place where Moses died after seeing the Promised Land from afar, and there he is probably buried, though the Mussulmans hold another site in veneration, on the opposite shore, as the supposed place of his sepulture. To the left of the range are the passes by which the Israelites entered the valley of the Jordan. In the foreground of the picture a green spot marks the valley of Jericho, famed in olden times for its beautiful gardens, but now a wilderness, and a breeding place of scorpions. Here was the Jericho of Christ's time ; the earlier city spoken of by the prophets was more to the left.

4. Jacob's Well.
6¼ x 9

The spot of land on which the well is dug was granted by the patriarch to his son Joseph. It lies in a deep valley at the foot of Mount Gerizim, before the entrance to the pass of Nablus, the ancient Sikkhim, once the capital of Samaria.

The ground over the well is raised, a Crusaders' church having once stood there; but of this nothing remains but a half-ruined arch over the well itself.

This is doubtless the well at which Christ was resting when he conversed with the woman of Samaria. "What might have been our Saviour's thoughts as He sat thus at the well, wearied with His journey? Perhaps He was thinking of Abraham, who built his first altar in the land in this opening of the plain (Gen. xi., 6), or of Jacob, whose only possession in the Land of Promise was here (xxxiii., 19). And even this possession, bought and paid for as it had been, was taken from him by the Amorites. But he reconquered it from them—'I took it out of the hand of the Amorite with my sword and my bow,' said the dying patriarch (Gen. xlviii., 22)—and left it to Joseph, who long years afterwards gave commandment concerning his bones, which were brought from Egypt and buried here (Joshua xxiv., 32). Perhaps Christ thought of Joseph wandering in that very field in search of his brethren (Gen. xxxvii., 15), and saw in the persecution of his brethren and the final victory of the beloved son, one of the divine pictures of the past, typical of Himself; or perhaps his thoughts were · dwelling upon that first gathering of all Israel when first they came into the land. . . ." (*Hodder.*)

5. The Tomb of Joseph.
6¼ x 5¼

Not far from the well is in all probability the real burial place of the celebrated minister of Pharaoh. It is well known that Joseph on his deathbed took the oath of the children of Israel, saying, "God will surely visit you, and ye shall carry up my bones from hence" (Gen. l., 25). "And the bones of Joseph which the children of Israel brought up out of Egypt, buried they in Shechem, in a parcel of ground which Jacob bought of the sons of Kamor, the father of Shechem.   . ." (Joshua xxiv., 32).

6. Gilgal.
4 x 6

The place in the Jordan valley where, as it is said, the Israelites, after crossing this river, erected the twelve stones and rested the first time in the Promised Land the Ark of the Covenant (Joshua iv., 19, 20). Here they celebrated for the first time the Passover.   Here Saul was anointed king. Here, too, the tribe of Judah welcomed David on his return from exile.

In the time of the early Christians there was a church here dedicated to the Archangel Michael, who appeared to Joshua at this spot—"a man over against him with his sword drawn in his hand, and Joshua went to him and said, ' Art thou for us or for our adversaries ?' And he said, ' Nay, but as captain of the host of the Lord an' I now come '" (Joshua v., 19), and inspired the Jews with courage to attack Jericho.

A solitary tamarisk now marks the spot, and some hillocks indicate the sites of Christian churches.

7. Samuel's Tomb.
4½ x 6½

It is not well known if this really be the burial-place of the great Israelitish judge.   The Mohammedans hold the place in the greatest honor, and visit it in thousands.   The tomb occupies a commanding site in the neighborhood of Jerusalem.   Here the Israelites assembled at Samuel's call to make war against the Philistines, and here they elected their first king.

All the neighboring heights and valleys are full of historical reminiscences.   The mount slopes down to the valley of Gabaon (Gibeon) where, before the battle between the tribes of Judah and Benjamin, twelve youths from either side fought with such ardor that they all fell dead (2 Samuel ii., 16).

In Gabaon also, Solomon sacrificed to God full a thousand men. Here the Lord appeared to him in a dream, promising to fulfil the wish of his heart, and to Solomon's desire for wisdom, joined riches and glory. Near here is the celebrated valley of Bethhoron, where the Israelites, under Joshua, vanquished the Amorites. He applied to the Lord, and cried out before the whole of Israel, " Sun, stand thou still upon Gibeon, and thou, Moon, in the valley of Ajalon " (Joshua x., 12). And the sun stood still and the moon stayed till Adonizedec, King of Jerusalem, was vanquished.

8. Gideon's Spring.

3 × 5

The rocky cavern whence issues water of the fountain, clear as crystal. Near this place a celebrated battle was fought ; Gideon with his three hundred warriors vanquished the host of the Midianites. At this spring he tried the bearing of his warriors by taking those only with him in his dangerous night expedition who, on coming to the spring after the hard day's march, drank water with the hands, and not those who bowed on the knees and drank with the mouth only.

It was night, and the Midianites were asleep. "The Midianites and the Amalekites and all the children of the East lay along in the valleys like grasshoppers for multitude, and their camels were without number as the sand by the sea-side for multitude. . . . And he divided the three hundred men into three companies, and he put a trumpet in every man's hand, with empty pitchers, and lamps within the pitchers" (Judges vii., 12, 16). So he drew near the camp of the Midianites. And at the moment the trumpets were blown and the pitchers broken, the Israelites holding the lamps with their left hands and the trumpets with their right, fell upon the panic-stricken foe with the cry, "The sword of the Lord and of Gideon" (Judges chap. vii.).

9. The Valley of Ezdraelon.

3 x 8½

This celebrated valley often witnessed the Israelitish struggles. On the right is Mount Gilboa, where Saul and his three sons were killed. On the left of Gilboa are the ruins of Jezreel, the residence of Ahab and Jezebel, where the latter was thrown from a window to the dogs. On the left of the small study one may see little Hermon, where the Philistines pitched camp before the battle against Saul; the Israelites occupied a position under Gilboa, near Gideon's spring; their position was bad, because the ground slopes towards the fountain, and thus gave the advantage to the Philistines. These put the Israelites to flight at once, so that the chief slaughter was probably on the heights, where the following day the bodies of Saul and his sons were found.

10. The Cave Endor.

Before the battle, as we know, Saul went to consult the Witch of Endor. His mission was not without danger, as the village of Endor is on the north side of little Hermon, at the foot of which was the camp of the Philistines. Saul turned to the right, and so could reach Endor "in two

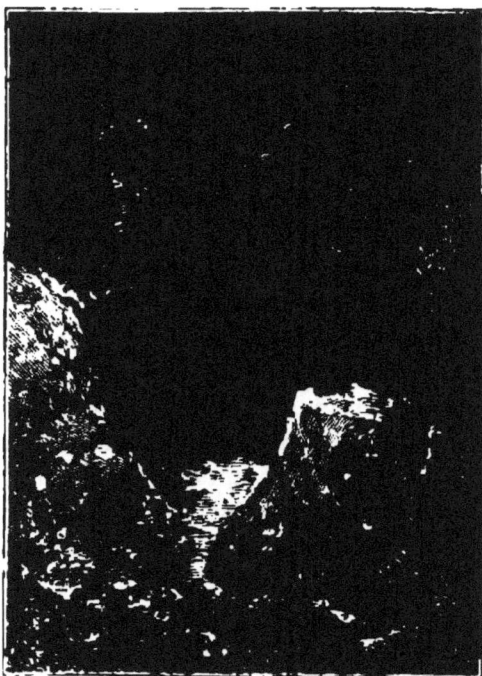

4! × 3

hours' time." The witch predicted to the King his defeat and death. "And to-morrow shalt thou and thy sons be with me : " (said the spirit of Samuel to the King), "the Lord also shall deliver the host of Israel into the hands of the Philistines " (1 Samuel xxviii., 19).

In the now very dirty village of Endor there are many caverns—possibly one of these was inhabited by the witch. Before the entrance of the cave here represented, traces of a threshold may be seen ; inside is a large room and another smaller beyond.

11. Beisan (Beth-shan).

3 x 6

The small green hill, seen in the distance, was the acropolis of an inaccessible fortress of the Philistines, the only one which the Israelites could never capture. The citadel stood on the summit of the hill, and from a near point of view appears to be naturally of uncommon strength. Deep ditches and a wall surround it. The principal gates, now almost in ruins, may still be seen on the north side, and it is not improbable that on these very gates were suspended the bodies of Saul and Jonathan, killed on the adjacent heights of Gilboa. "And it came to pass on the morrow, when the Philistines came to strip the slain, that they found Saul and his three sons fallen in Mount Gilboa. And they cut off his head and stripped off his armour, and sent into the land of the Philistines round about, to publish it in the house of their idols and among the people. And they put his armour in the house of Ashtaroth, and they fastened his body to the wall of Beth-shan " (1 Samuel xxxi., 8–10).

12. Beisan (Beth-shan) Theatre.

3½ x 5½

The same hill forms one side of a Roman theater, now completely overgrown with bushes, but the doors and passages are still well preserved. The building is semi-circular and entirely built of blocks of basalt. A great number of Christians, especially during the reign of Julian, were torn to pieces here by wild beasts.

13. Solomon's Wall.

18 x 23½

The six lower ranges of these splendid stones are beyond doubt of the time of David and Solomon, the next rows may be attributed to Herod, while the upper and smallest date from the Mohammedan period. This part of the great wall which surrounded the Temple is called *The Wailing Place*, because the Jews for a long time past have been in the habit of coming hither—at first once a year on the anniversary of the destruction of Jerusalem (on payment of a heavy tax to the Mussulman authorities), and in more recent days as frequently as they wished—to bewail their past greatness and present dispersion. Seldom can anything more touching be seen. The Jews of both sexes and of all ages arrive from all parts of the world to pray and weep with loud cries, and literally to wash with their tears the sacred stones ! On Friday the place is quite full of people from Palestine, Central Asia, India, Europe and especially from Russia—all praying in the most plaintive tones, beating their breasts, rocking their bodies to and fro, or leaning motionless against the stones and weeping, weeping, weeping !

The Jews seem to bring all their sorrows and misfortunes to this place. A woman approaches with unsteady gait, throws herself against the wall, and in an agonized voice implores God to give her back her dead child. Farther on two Jews, wearied with praying, are talking business. " Have you bought ? What have you paid ? Too dear !" and so on. After this interlude they recommence praying and weeping.

An old rabbi is sitting in his corner on a stone or an empty wine box with the inevitable " Bordeaux " mark, and with eyes full of tears reads in his book : " O God, the heathen are come into thine inheritance ; thy holy temple have they defiled ; they have laid Jerusalem in heaps. . . .

No. 13. SOLOMON'S WALL.

We are become a reproach to our neighbours, a scorn and derision to them that are round about us. How long, Lord? Will'st thou be angry with us for ever! Shall thy jealousy burn like fire?"

Fragments of an interesting litany are often sung here:

I.

Reader: Because of the palace which is deserted,
People: We sit alone and weep.
Reader: Because of the Temple which is destroyed,
Because of the walls which are broken down,
Because of our greatness which is departed,
Because of the precious stones of the Temple ground to powder,
Because of our priests who have erred and gone astray.
Because of our kings who have contemned God,
People: We sit alone and weep.

II.

Reader: We beseech Thee. have mercy on Zion.
People: And gather together the children of Jerusalem.
Reader: Make speed, make speed, O Deliverer of Zion.
People: Speak after the heart of Jerusalem.
Reader: Let Zion be girded with beauty and with majesty.
People: Show favour unto Jerusalem.
Reader: Let Zion find again her kings.
People: Comfort those who mourn over Jerusalem.
Reader: Let peace and joy return to Jerusalem.
People: Let the branch of Jerusalem put forth and bud.

(*See also No. 94.*)

14. Business and Prayers.

10 x 6½

15. The Spring of Elisha.

6 x 9

Most probably the spring whose bitter water the prophet made sweet in answer to the complaint of the inhabitants: "And the men of the city said unto Elisha, Behold, I pray thee, the situation of this city is pleasant, as my Lord seeth; but the water is naught and the ground barren. And he said, bring me a new cruse, and put salt therein. And they brought it to him. And he went forth unto the spring of the waters and cast the salt in there, and said, Thus saith the Lord, I have healed these waters ; there shall not be from them any more death or barren land. So the waters were healed unto this day, according to the saying of Elisha which he spake " (2 Kings ii., 19–23).

Under the spring are the remains of a wall of Roman date. It is generally admitted that Herod drowned in this spring his relative Aristobulus, upon whom the people looked as his successor.

16. Ruins of a Samaritan Temple at Shechem.

6¼ x 9

When the Jews returned from captivity in Babylon, the Samaritans, who "feared the Lord but served their own gods," desired to assist them in rebuilding the temple but were refused. They then resolved to build one for themselves on Mount Gerizim, and their hostility to the Jews increased to such a point that it became a sin to extend the rites of hospitality on either side, and the words of the woman of Samaria to Christ expressed well the feeling which afterwards existed between the two races : " How is it that thou, being a Jew, askest drink of me who am a woman of Samaria? for the Jews have no dealings with the Samaritans." The temple on Mount Gerizim was destroyed later, and on the place where it stood, probably out of the same materials, was built a church dedicated to the Virgin, also now in ruins. The walls are thick and the stones very large. Some of these stones, of unusual size, are identified, according to the legend, with the twelve stones brought from the Jordan and erected at Gilgal as a memorial, but this is highly improbable. Even more dubious is the assertion of the Samaritans that Abraham offered up Isaac at this spot, and that Jacob had here the vision of the heavenly ladder, etc., etc.

The Samaritans to the present day celebrate their Passover here with offerings, and the entire ceremonial as in
olden times. It may be remarked that their numbers are
ve.y small, some fifty souls at the most, and they are constantly diminishing. I have not had the opportunity of
sketching one of their types, but find them very like the
Jews in appearance. The summit of Mount Gerizim is
nearly three thousand feet above sea level. The view from
the table land and the ruins is beautiful. On one side may
be seen the Mediterranean, and on the other, the snowy
crest of Hermon.

17. An Old Street in Samaria, Sebastia.
4½ x 5½

Under the reign of Asa, King of Judah, Omri, King of
Israel, bought the hill Samaria, for two talents of silver, built
a city, and removed thither his residence from Shechem.
His son Ahab, who married Jezebel, introduced again the
worship of Baal. " And he reared up an altar for Baal, in the
house of Baal, which he had built in Samaria. And Ahab
made a grove, and Ahab did more to provoke the Lord God
of Israel to anger than all the kings of Israel that were
before him " (1 Kings xvi., 30-32). At a later date the
miracles of Elisha took place here.

Herod entirely rebuilt the city, embellished it and called
it, in honor of the Emperor Agustus, Sebastia. The columns
now remaining belong to this period. These noble survivors of the past magnificence of the place, rearing aloft
above the corn-fields, appeal powerfully to the imagination.
Looking upon the desolate scene one is reminded of the
words of the prophecy : " Samaria shall become desolate for
she hath rebelled against her God " (Hosea xiii., 16). " I will
make Samaria as an heap of the field and as plantings of a vine-
yard, and I will pour down the stones thereof into the valley,
and I will discover the foundations thereof " (Micah i.. 6).

18. Entrance to the Tombs of the Kings.
23½ x 18

Near Jerusalem, on the road to Damascus, a large
monumental staircase, cut in the rock, leads to an entrance
which was lately thoroughly excavated. (It is easy to see
on the picture that part of the rock which remained for
centuries under the earth.)

This entrance opens on a large court, surrounded by
rocks of very imposing character. The waters are led away
to cisterns, which, like the whole work, are of a coarse but
solid structure.

19. Tombs of the Kings.
18 x 23½

In this court (see last picture) is a wide vestibule,
formerly surported by two columns, of which next to
nothing remains. Under the opening is a long sculptured
frieze, of excellent taste, with the traditional bunch of grapes,
emblem of the Promised Land. A fine cornice over it is
unfortunately much injured. The learned Frenchman, De
Saulcy, was of opinion that here were the tombs of the
Israelite kings; he supposed also that the sarcophagus
which he found here was that of David; but both suppo-
sitions are incorrect, and now it is admitted that Helena,
Princess of Adiabene, who became a convert to Judaism, was
buried here with her family, about the beginning of our
era.

In the course of his excavations De Saulcy found here
many urns, vases, and lamps of Roman date, some small
vases of oriental alabaster, some caskets of precious stones
and gold ornaments. He found also a room previously
unknown, containing a sarcophagus with a human corpse
inside. On first opening it the body was found well preserved, but it crumbled away almost immediately. The
tomb contains many low rooms surrounded by niches in

which the bodies of Helena's numerous family were laid. Most curious is the entrance stone, so constructed that a thief or any one who did not know the secret might enter, but could not come out.　He would be buried alive !

20. A Fountain near Nazareth.

3¼ x 6¼

A very old one, dating from the early years of our era, and doubtless visited by Christ and His brethren on their way to and from Nazareth.　It is half way between Nazareth and Kefr-Cama, the Cana of Galilee, where the miracle of turning water into wine was performed, and where are shown at the present day the very vessels which served for this miracle (!)

21. That Part of Jordan where Christ was Baptized.

5 x 6¼

The bed of the river is only about a hundred feet wide ; the stream, however is very rapid, and looks treacherous— nearly every year it carries off some careless worshippers, deceived by its quiet, calm surface.　The shores are covered with willow, tamarisk, and oleander trees, in whose thickets lurk the wild boar, the panther, and occasionally a Bedouin robber.　As in the times of Christ, this locality is the resort of runaways and fugitives from the police, so that it is never considered quite safe.　Many efforts have been made to mark out the exact place where the Israelites crossed the Jordan, but the question is far from decided even now, the river having several times changed its bed.

It was hereabouts that the prophet Elijah divided the waters, crossed the dry bed of the river, and was taken up to heaven.　Here, too, Elisha divided the river with the mantle of his master and the words : " Where is the God of Elijah !"　The main interest, however, centres round one of the greatest events of the New Testament, the baptism of

Christ by John, which according to tradition took place here. "Then cometh Jesus from Galilee to Jordan unto John, to be baptized of him." "And Jesus when he was baptized, went up straightway out of the water : and lo, the heavens were opened unto him, and he saw the spirit of God descending like a dove and lighting upon him : and lo, a voice from heaven, saying, This is my beloved Son in whom I am well pleased " (Matt. iii., 13, 16, 17).

Every year great numbers of worshippers visit the river : Greeks, Russians, and others precisely at this spot, the Latins a little farther down. The former gather in great caravans, and on the 18th January, men and women old and young, sink into the holy stream, where a strong rope is fastened for the purpose. Nobody pays any attention to personal appearance after this bath, salvation being the only thought of the moment.

22. Capernaum (Tell-Hum).
4 x 6½

A melancholy place on the north coast of the Sea of Tiberias. Immediately behind the little hut shown on the study are ruins of a most imposing character, probably the finest both in size and beauty of workmanship to be found in Palestine. Overgrown with tall grass and weeds are lying huge blocks of white marble splendidly ornamented, capitals of pillars, architraves, etc.

Wilson says in his book : If Tell-Hum be Capernaum, this is without a doubt the synagogue built by the Roman centurion, and one of the most sacred places on earth. It was in this building that our Lord gave the discussion on the Bread of Life (John vi.). " These things said he in the synagogue as he taught in Capernaum." In Capernaum Christ passed three years of his life and had "his own house." " And leaving Nazareth he came and dwelt in Capernaum which is upon the sea-coast, in the borders of

Zabulon and Nephthalim; that it might be fulfilled which was spoken by Esias the prophet, saying: The land of Zabulon and the land of Nephthalim by the way of the sea, beyond Jordan, Galilee of the Gentiles; the people which sat in darkness saw great light; and to them which sat in the region and shadow of death, light is sprung up" (Matt. iv., 13–16).

Among the miracles performed here were the healing the paralyzed man, the healing of the mother-in-law of the Apostle Peter, of the centurion's servant, and so on.

It has been supposed that these are the ruins of Chorazin, but tradition is strongly against this idea.

23. Bethsaida.
4 x 6½

The home of the Apostles Peter, Andrew, Philip, James, and John. "And is came to pass that as the people pressed upon him to hear the word of God, he stood by the lake of Gennesaret and saw two ships standing by the lake; but the fishermen were gone out of them and were washing their nets" (Luke v., 1). He entered into Simon's ship and taught the people on shore, and afterward performed the miracle of the draught of fishes which astonished Peter, James, and John; and the Master said unto them: "Fear not, from henceforth thou shalt catch men. And when they had brought their ships to shore, they forsook all and followed Him" (Luke v., 11). Here the blind man received his sight, and on a height in the vicinity was performed the miracle of the multiplication of loaves.

No other part of the sea-coast is so convenient for fishing as this small bay with its low sandy bank. Even now fishermen are living here. On our demand they immediately drew their nets and caught some fine fish. Here and there are seen heights of waste ground under which would probably be found some interesting remains.

24. Mount Tabor.

3½ x 5½

Of very regular form, rises to the height of 2,362 feet above sea-level. On the summit are ruins of a fortress of ancient date, so that it is nearly impossible to suppose that the Saviour chose this spot for the transfiguration ; indeed, it is only from the time of Jerome, or the fourth century, that Tabor is accepted as the place of the miracle which, with more probability, may be assigned to any other " high mountain apart," the only words of the New Testament indicating the place of the event.

25. The Summit of Tabor.

2¼ x 6½

There are ruins of two churches of the Crusaders' time. The Catholic monks to whom they belong intend to restore the once splendid buildings. The view from this point is beautiful.

26. Entrance to the Grotto of the Mount of Temptation.

10½ x 6

From time out of mind this mountain was pierced with grottoes of anchorites, and there is a very probable tradi- tion, according to which Christ passed in one of these grot- toes His forty days of fasting and prayer. On the summit, at the place where it is said our Saviour was tempted by the devil, are still the ruins of a church attributed to the Empress Helena : " And the devil taking him up into a high mountain showed unto him all the kingdoms of the world in a moment of time." The entrance to the grotto is half-way up the mountain. A road now is made instead of the old path from which pilgrims sometimes fell into the abyss below.

A Greek monk is the only inhabitant of this grotto. When not engaged in prayer he diverts himself by feeding

No. 26. ENTRANCE TO THE GROTTO OF THE MOUNT OF
TEMPTATION.

the only living creatures of the neighborhood—blackbirds, which catch the bits of dried fruits thrown to them.

27. The Mount of Temptation by Night.
9 x 6

In the night, when a light burns in the grotto, the imagination is carried back 1854 years, when the Great Anchorite prepared His poor food, or prayed and meditated on His future deeds and destiny. More than once, probably, the devil came to tempt Him and make Him doubt whether the only possible way before Him was that which led through a shameful death on the Cross.

28. Kitchen of the Monks in the Grotto.
9½ x 6½

The hermit monks are most abstemious ; their diet consisting of black bread of a very coarse kind, beans, onions, garlic, and olives. They nevertheless find means to help the poor Bedouins in their necessities.

29. Refectory of the Grotto.
8 x 14

The walls were once covered with frescoes, but of these scarcely anything remains. A door opens on a balcony whence there is a really charming and interesting view over the Jordan valley. Just in front is Jericho ; further on a line of vegetation shows the direction of the Jordan, with the monastery of St. John. On the right is the Dead Sea, with the monastery holy Gerasimus, built, it is believed on the spot where the Virgin Mary rested on her way to Egypt (?). On the left is the Jordan valley with the road leading to Tiberias and the mountains of Samaria.

30. The part of the Grotto which according to tradition dates from the time of Christ.
10½ x 7

From early Christian times this part of the grotto was converted into a chapel and was venerated as the place where our Saviour set the example of retreat, fasting and penitence. "And Jesus being full of the Holy Ghost returned from Jordan and was led by the spirit into the wilderness, being forty days tempted by the devil. And in those days he did eat nothing ; and when they were ended he afterward hungered." (Luke iv., 1–2.)

31. The Cupola of the Holy Sepulchre in Jerusalem.

2½ x 6

This was many times destroyed by fire and rebuilt. As it stands at present it was erected at the cost of the Russian, French, and Turkish governments in 1869. The diameter of the cupola is 78.7 feet.

On the western side of the Sepulchre Church the ruins of the Basilica of the Emperor Constantine were discovered some years ago by the Russian archimandrite, Antonin, and apparently also the foundation of a city gate, by which possibly our Saviour was led to execution.

32. One of the old Jewish Tombs near Jerusalem.

10 x 12

An extremely low entrance leads to a small, very low room in the rock, wherein are many niches for corpses. In one of such niches, never before used, was interred the body of Christ, in a rock near Golgotha where Joseph of Arimathea, possibly, had his family tomb. The entrance was usually closed with a big stone, and it was impossible to enter or come out otherwise than by the small aperture seen on the study.

Such are all the tombs of those times ; there was no other style ; and if at present the grave of our Saviour has the form of a box, it is because the rock over it has been broken off, partly for the necessities of worship, partly by the worshipers themselves for relics.

32

33. An Arab Woman.
11 x 8

The type of the Arab woman may be called beautiful. It is common to meet women at places of public resort of striking beauty ; but, like all Oriental women, they grow old very early. The poorer Arab women work very hard, while the rich look upon every kind of work as degrading, and pass their days in incessant chatter.

34. A Court of a House in Jerusalem.
10½ x 12

A characteristic old building near Solomon's Wall, such as are ordinarily occupied by two or three families, who are constantly quarreling among themselves. While engaged at my work, I heard an incessant clatter proceeding from the shrill voices of women, mingled with occasional cries of children, the men very seldom interfering in these disputes. To make matters worse, the atmosphere in these picturesque courts was often insupportable from bad smells, and many of the children were suffering from different contagious disorders, such as small-pox.

35. The Holy Family, as I understand it, according to the following texts of the Gospel :

Matthew i., 25 ; xii., 46, 47, 48 ; xiii., 55, 56.—Mark iii., 31, 32, 33, 34, 55 ; vi., 3.—John ii., 12 ; vii., 3, 5, 10.

37½ x 47

36. Jesus with John the Baptist on the Jordan.
28 x 47

" Then cometh Jesus from Galilee to Jordan unto John to be baptised of him " (Matthew iii., 13). John vowed himself to the Lord ; he neither cut his hair nor drank wine ; from his youth he withdrew to the desert, where he lived in the most ascetic manner. "And John was clothed with camels' hair, and with a girdle of a skin about his loins, and he did eat locusts and wild honey " (Mark i., 6).

He was an ascetic, resembling those ascetics who may still be seen in India, whence most probably the type came over to Judæa. The people regarded him as a Prophet or even as a Messiah, and for a long time the Priests and the Pharisees dared not undertake anything against him, notwithstanding his bold and loud condemnations of their life and rules.

The people streamed to him to be baptised, as the sign of the adoption of the new principles. Christ, who at that time was very little known, came also to John, and was baptised with the others.

" The next day John seeth Jesus coming unto him, and saith, ' Behold the Lamb of God, which taketh away the sin of the world. This is he of whom I said, after me cometh a man which is preferred before me, for he was before me ' " (John i., 29, 30). " Now when John had heard in the prison the works of Christ, he sent two of his disciples and said unto him, ' Art thou He that should come, or do we look for another ' " (Matthew xi., 2, 3). " And as they departed, Jesus began to say unto the multitudes concerning John, ' What went ye out into the wilderness to see ? . . . A prophet ? Yea, I say unto you and more than a prophet. For this is he of whom it is written ' " (Matthew xi., 7, 9, 10).

37. Jesus in the Desert.

30 x 48

" The spirit driveth him into the wilderness, and he was there in the wilderness forty days, tempted of Satan " (Mark i., 12, 13).

Possibly Christ, on returning from Jordan, remained forty days in the desert in one of the numerous old grottoes of the so-called Mount Quarantania, and left the retreat only after hearing of John's imprisonment. Many times afterwards He

No. 38. CHRIST ON THE SEA OF TIBERIAS.

No. 39. THE PROPHECY.

retired to the desert, partly for safety, partly to meditate and compose his thoughts. . . .

From the statement of contemporaries it is known that our Saviour had a handsome figure, beautiful blond hair—auburn, according to Bysantic tradition.

He seldom smiled but was easily moved to tears.

Women were greatly devoted to Him, and He was often followed by a number of them. His face was beautiful according to some, while the others testify quite to the contrary (Tertullian).

38. Christic on the Sea of Tiberias.
20 x 40

Jesus went out of his house, and sat by the sea-side. And great multitudes were gathered unto him, so that he went into a ship and sat ; and the whole multitude stood on the shore " (Matthew xiii., 1, 2).

"And it came to pass that as the people pressed upon him to hear the word of God, he stood by the lake of Gennesaret. . . ." (Luke v., 1, 2, 3).

39. The Prophecy.
29 x 39

"Then began he to upbraid the cities wherein most of his mighty works were done, because they repented not: "Woe unto thee, Chorazin! woe unto thee, Bethsaida! for if the mighty works which were done in you, had been done in Tyra and Sidon, they would have repented long ago in sackcloth and ashes. But I say unto you, it shall be more tolerable for Tyre and Sidon at the day of judgment than for you. And thou, Capernaum, which art exalted unto heaven, shall be brought down to hell, for if the mighty works which have been done in thee, had been done in Sodom, it would have remained unto this day. But I say unto you that it shall be more tolerable for the land of

No. 41.   THE CHIEF MOSQUE IN FUTTEHPORE.

Sodom in the day of judgment than for thee " (Matt. xi., 20-24).

It is to be remarked that now not only in the desolation of these sites, but in the very dispute about their identity, it had indeed been "more tolerable for Tyre and Sidon " in the day of their earthly judgment than for those cities: the names of Tyre and Sidon are preserved, their sites are unquestioned, but here the names are gone, and the cities problematical.

40. The House of Berbul in Futtehpore Sikri (in the neighborhood of Agra).

17½ x 23½

So massive are the red stone buildings, so fine and delicate their details, that from the outside, as well as from the interior, the structure seems carved out of ivory. Raja Berbul, favorite of the great Mogul Akbar, was one of the adherents of the party who contemplated a fusion of Saracenic with Indian elements, and this building bears witness to his intentions.

41. The Chief Mosque in Futtehpore Sikri

18 x 23½

Stands on the western side of an immense courtyard, surrounded by beautiful galleries, with many other mosques and enormous gates.

Built after the pattern of the mosque in Mekka, erected over the grave of Mahomet, entrance to which is strictly forbidden to unbelievers.

42. The Pearl Mosque in Agra.

18 x 23½

The temple is of white marble in Mauresque style, of very fine proportions. There are few or no ornaments, but the beauty of lines and of the material compensate for it. The mosque was built in the year 1654, at the time when the first signs of decay in the Mogul art began to be felt.

43. Sunrise in the Himalayas.

25 x 18

Opposite Darjiling. Sunrise and sunset in these mountains afford the most ravishing and magnificent sights which the brush can only approximately depict.

One day I went out to make a sketch of the sunset. I prepared my palette, but the sight was so beautiful I waited, delayed the work in order to examine better the sight. Several thousand feet below me all was wrapt in a pure blue shadow ; the summits of the peaks were resplendent in purple flames. I waited, and waited, and would not begin my sketch. " By and by," said I, "I want to look at it still, it is so splendid ! " I continued to wait, and waited until the end of the evening—until the sun was set, and the mountains were enveloped in dark shadows. Then I shut up my paintbox and returned home.

44. The same.

5 x 8

45. The Taj in the Morning (from the Garden).

15 x 21½

46. The Taj in the Evening (from the Garden).

23 x 17½

47. The Taj in the Evening (from the River).

18 x 24

The Taj is properly a monument erected by the Great Mogul, Shah Jihan, over the grave of his favorite wife. She died in full strength of youth and beauty, and the Great

Mogul promised in memory of her to build such a monument over her tomb that would surpass all the existing constructions. And so he did. I must say that in my opinion there is nothing even in Europe which can surpass the Taj —this quiet, solemn, wonderful place of the last rest of a charming woman, who died giving birth to her first child, the future emperor. Built of white marble, it is decked from top to bottom with ornaments of lapis-lazuli, malachite, cornelians, and other precious stones. It is difficult to form an idea of the splendor of this building without seeing it. From the garden it affords a particularly charming aspect, where its beautiful lines and dazzling white marble are thrown into high relief by the dark green foliage.

There were 20,000 men engaged upon it for seventeen years, and although the labor cost nothing, the sum of $20,000,000 was swallowed up by this building.

The entrance door was made of massive silver, and an enormous diamond was placed on the tomb itself. One may remark, perhaps, that the middle cupola is a little too heavy, or that some other details could have been treated in another way, but taken in its ensemble, as I remarked somewhere before, Taj can be compared to a beautiful woman whom you make bold to criticise when she is absent, but in whose presence you can only say : Charming, charming, charming !

48. Mount Kanchinjinga, from Darjiling in the Evening.

24 X 17

49. Thibetan Lamas.

10 X 8

Good-natured, voracious creatures, who never change their clothes, which therefore smell, and are full of insects. Nevertheless, all the higher Lamas are immortal, *i.e.,* their souls, according to the Buddhist belief, are immediately after death born again in the bodies of little children.

50. Hindu Workman.

10 x 9½

Down-trodden, poor beings, who can never quite satisfy their hunger. The Hindu is remarkable for his talent for any work requiring great patience. Builder of the greatest and most handsome monuments, accomplished workman in the finest jewelry work, hard worker in every line—he lives on five cents a day, himself and family. When the hard time of famine comes on he only tightens his belt, compressing his stomach more and more every day.

51. Bhutanese of Sikkhim in the Himalayas.

10½ x 8

The Bhutanese are of Mongol race ; an idle, quarrelsome, and. extremely superstitious people. The tribe is closely connected with Thibet, properly speaking : and these men are very numerous in the Thibetan army the English have to face in their present war.

52. Bhutanese Girl.

8 x 5½

53. Bhutanese Woman.

8 x 6

54. Kanchinjinga, Pandim and other Mountains in the Clouds.

18 x 25

These effects of sun in India are simply astonishing ; without seeing them it is difficult to have faith in the truthfulness of the artist.

55. Sunset in India.

13¼ x 7½

56. The Gate of Allah-Uddin in Ancient Delhi.

9⅝ x 12½

Has been built upwards of six hundred years, of red sandstone admirably preserved. Court attendants, and grooms with horses, await the coming of their master.

SECOND NIGHT'S SALE.

WEDNESDAY, NOVEMBER 18th,

BEGINNING PROMPTLY AT 8 O'CLOCK

RUSSIAN TYPES.

1 30 **57. Blacksmith,** native of Vladimir, 59 years of age.

13½ x 10

125 **58. His Wife,** 50 years of age.

11½ x 10½

59. Coppersmith, native of Smolensk, 62 years of age,
115 has all his life made cockades.

12½ x 10½

400 **60. Girl of District near Mosko,** 15 years of age.

14 x 12

120 **61. Dvornik (gate-keeper),** 40 years of age, native of
Rjazan.

12 x 10½

62. Retired Valet de Chambre, 70 years of age, has
been 50 years in service, and looks upon his masters with
feelings not unmixed with irony.

150   12 x 11

1 1 #

1040

63. Mendicant Friar of the Order of Nakhsb-bendi at
the doors of a Mosque in Turkestan.

350

24 X 19

155 **64. The Kreml of Moscow in Winter.**

10 X 13

195 **65. The same.**

66. The Moscow Cathedrals and the river Moskva
(in the spring).

315

15 X 18½

250 *66 — study — Read —*

67. A Street in the Town of Rostov, in the winter,
with the setting sun.

9 X 12

530

**68. Jkonostass of an old Wooden Church in the
Village of Jshna.**

13½ X 10½

Services are rarely held in this church. Therefore it is
preserved as it was in the XVIIth century. It has escaped
the hands of the restorers and of the lovers of modern
sumptuosities.

380 **69. Interior of same Church.**

15 X 11

This is the Prior's Pew, the church having formerly
belonged to a monastery.

A Jew of Jerusalem.

70. Entrance Door of the same Church.

12 X 7

Together with ·the good old woman who, in place of her
octogenarian husband, takes care of the church and protects
it against embellishments.

71. Ancient Terems (palaces) in the Kreml of Rostov.

13½ x 15½

These palaces were occupied by the Dukes of Rostov;
after them by the metropolitans of the province; and,
among others, by Philaret, father of the first Tsar of the
house of Romanof, who was forced to take orders by
another pretender to the throne, a more powerful man,
Godunof, who succeeded in getting into power for a short
time.

72. Entrance Door to the Ipatief Cathedral at Kostroma.

13 X 10½

At this door came out the first Romanof, the Tsar
Michel Feodorovitch, when he showed himself to the people
after his election. The young prince was hiding, together
with his mother, behind the walls of the monastery, from the
Poles, who devastated Russia at that time; and it was here
that he received the delegated who came solemnly offering
the crown to him.

73. Family Vault of the Soltykofs and other princely families in the monastery of Bogojavlensk in Kostroma.

10½ X 13½

74. The Portico of a Church of the XVIIth Century in Jaroslexv.

17 X 23

It is on such galleries that, waiting for the service to begin, or at the end of it, the people come out to rest themselves and to converse. The vaults and the walls are covered with paintings on subjects from the Holy Writ, with appropriate inscriptions.

75. The Same.

17 X 25

76. Before Sunrise. A Lake in Cashmere.

60 x 86

77. After Sunset. A small lake near Delhi.

58 x 78

78. The Night. My fire in the Himalayas.

79 X 59

79. Mount Chattin.

4 X 7

This is the summit of a rock on the way from Nazareth to Tiberias, remarkable as the scene of the last battle fought between the Crusaders and the Mussulmans, which decided the fate of Christendom in the Holy Land. Seven hundred years ago, on the 14th July, 1187, Saladin vanquished the Christians under the command of King Lusinian, who allowed himself to be enticed to this rock from a good position he had occupied on the road to Nazareth. After a march of twenty-four hours, during which the knights were harassed by heat, hunger, thirst, and constant alarms, the

Christian army took up their position for the night on this field, and were at once surrounded by the enemy, so that by the following morning the issue of the battle was already decided. The heavily armed and wearied knights on their tired horses could not withstand the light bodies of Arabs, and were very soon forced to retire to the summit of the rock (shown on the sketch). Here the king, surrounded by the clergy, high officials, and officers, surrendered after a desperate defense.

80. The Hermits on the Jordan.

8 x 7

These hermits, who are not numerous, live partly on the shore itself, partly on the sandstone hills some distance off, near the monastery of St. John. They excavate caves with two or three rooms in each, so small that it is difficult to turn round in them. These holes are usually covered with images, crosses, etc.; they are warm in winter and cool in summer. The only inconvenience is the great number of mosquitoes of all sizes, down to some so small as to be nearly imperceptible. Those who inhabit caves on the shores complain of toads, snakes and other reptiles. The occupations of the hermits are praying, fishing, and turning crosses of sandal-wood, or tying woolen chaplets, etc., these objects being gladly bought by worshipers visiting the Sacred River.

81. Portrait of a Hermit.

13½ x 7

Still a young man, of steady appearance. He has served in the Church of Golgotha, but was obliged to abandon it, in order to avoid the example of the other monks in their free manners with the female worshipers.

82. A Russian Hermit.

190

12½ x 10

Father Vassian from Kamenetz Podolsk, in South Russia, formerly a miller by profession, is waiting for an opportunity to build a good mill for some cloister, and afterward to die in peace near the Sacred River. He was particularly pleased with the chaplets on the sketch, which serve him for his prayers, three times a day, morning, evening, and midnight, when he gives 300 points to Christ, 300 to the Virgin Mary, 200 to the Angels, Archangels, Prophets, and Apostles, and 200 to all the Saints ! His belief is great and sincere, but the devil evidently tempts him, as he asked me in confidence, " if the Tsar would see his portrait, and possibly give him some gratification."

83. His Lodging.

35

6½ x 5

On the summit of a hill, with a small canopy over the entrance. Passing worshipers lay at his door some trifling gift, such as biscuits or copper money.

St. John the Baptist probably lived in a similar hole. According to tradition he led a wandering life, and had two or three refuges on the other side of the river, more or less remote, according as his relations happened to be with the authorities.

84. Portrait of a Jewish Rabbi.

12 x 10

A Rabbi from the Western Provinces of Russia. The Jews, especially the aged, come in great numbers to the Holy City, in order to pass in it their last years, and to be buried in the valley of Jehosaphat, whence they believe they will be called before others to the future life. The Jewish population of Jerusalem has largely increased in latter years,

partly because of the great number of charitable institutions built and supported by Montefiore, the Rothschilds, and some other banker-kings. The Turkish government was so much alarmed by this invasion of Jews, that it issued an order forbidding them to remain in the Holy Land more than thirty days, and to settle there. The Turks are evidently afraid that the Promised Land will again pass into the possession of the Jews—and this will certainly happen some day.

This portrait was only obtained under a promise that it should not be hung in a Christian church.

85. A Rabbi.
13 x 10

Stipulated for a glass of brandy at each sitting.

86. A Rabbi.
9½ x 6½

87. Portrait of an Arab.
9½ x 6½

The Arabs came here with the Kalifs as conquerors. They have a good type, are hospitable, and belong mostly to the Sunni sect, of the Mohammedan religion. There are, however, many Christians now among them, large sums of money having been spent every year by different Christian sects to attract Arab families to their faith. Often after having accepted help from one community, the Arab returns to his former faith, or allows himself to be converted to another religion where the reward is more substantial. This rivalry between the different Christian faiths is the cause of great corruption in the character of modern Arabs in the Holy Land.

88. In Bulgaria during the War (Outposts in the Balkans.)
6 x 5

89. In Bulgaria after the War.
19 x 15

7900

90. Cossack Picket on the Danube.

30 x 66

Pickets of Cossacks and Hussars were stationed along the left bank of the Danube opposite Rustchuk, before the Russians crossed this river. At each Cossack picket was a beacon with tarred straw twisted round it, to be lighted in case of alarm, in order that danger might be at once signalled down the whole line.

91. The Earth Huts at Shipka.

23 x 31

The road up the Shipka Pass reminded me of a village. On one side were the earth huts of the soldiers, with an occasional small house of a commanding officer; on the other a row of fir tops to show the direction of the road in misty weather. Having no warm clothing, the men covered themselves with anything they could get, mostly bits of tent canvas which served instead of overcoats. This was a very slight protection against the cold, and large numbers were frostbitten every day. The close earth huts swarmed with every species of insect, and though bullet-proof to some extent, afforded no shelter against artillery fire, particularly shells, which often burst through the roofs and killed everybody inside. It was dangerous to venture outside the huts, owing to the commanding positions held by the Turks, who enfiladed our men on three sides, and could pick them off with their rifle fire. It became particularly lively at meal times, when the rations were brought round in troikas (carts drawn by three horses) from the shelter of the hills, and now and again a shell would burst in the midst of a crowd surrounding one of these provision wagons, and confuse in one heap, cart, horses, and men. The water-bearers also suffered heavily, many of them never returning. All day

No. 90.   COSSACK PICKET ON THE DANUBE.

long bullets were whizzing about, literally like flies ; every minute a shell would burst, now on this side, now on that. Well do I remember one day sitting down to sketch under cover of a Turkish bullet-proof block-house, and being obliged to leave my work unfinished, three shells in rapid succession having struck the roof, entered and broken everything, covering my palette thickly with dust and dirt.

92. Snow Trenches on the Pass.

46 x 78

The day of our crossing the Balkans, in order to guard against a possible flank attack, Skobeleff ordered trenches to be dug. The earth was so hard frozen that it became necessary to throw up breastworks of snow, which lay so deep on the ground that the Turks never thought of attacking us, but only assembled in crowds in their positions on our front, on a level with us, evidently surprised at our movements in the deep snow, while the few shells fired from their batteries caused us no loss. That night the frost was intense, and our soldiers having nothing but their thin overcoats to wear (the warm clothing did not arrive till spring) strict orders were given in the regiments that every one should be kept awake. Slumber that night meant death. I remember trying to doze near the camp-fire, protected with a number of warm wraps, yet in spite of all this I felt that I was freezing, and accordingly lit a cigar and waited by the fireside till it was time to march.

93. "All Quiet at Shipka !"

(*All Quiet along the Potomac.*)

(A series of three paintings, each 22 x 14.)

General Radetsky's report to the commander-in-chief. The daily losses from Turkish bullets were far exceeded by

No. 93. "All Quiet at Shipka"

those from frost-bite. Nearly the whole of the 24th divis-
ion was frost-bitten. Regiments were dreadfully reduced
in strength ; in some companies only ten men and a few
subalterns were left ; at length, the pitiable remnants were
withdrawn from position. The General reported as usual,
" All is quiet at Shipka ! "

94. Solomon's Wall.

75 x 59.

The six lower ranges of these splendid stones are beyond
doubt of the time of David and Solomon, the next rows
may be attributed to Herod, while the upper and smallest
date from the Mohammedan period. This part of the great
wall which surrounded the Temple is called *The Wailing
Place*, because the Jews for a long time past have been
in the habit of coming hither—at first once a year on the
anniversary of the destruction of Jerusalem (on payment
of a heavy tax to the Mussulman authorities), and in more
recent days as frequently as they wished—to bewail their
past greatness and present dispersion. Seldom can anything more touching be seen. The Jews of both sexes and
of all ages arrive from all parts of the world to pray and
weep with loud cries, and literally to wash with their tears
the sacred stones ! On Friday the place is quite full of
people from Palestine, Central Asia, India, Europe, and
especially from Russia—all praying in the most plaintive
tones, beating their breasts, rocking their bodies to and fro,
or leaning motionless against the stones and weeping, weeping, weeping !

The Jews seem to bring all their sorrows and misfortunes
to this place. A woman approaches with unsteady gait,
throws herself against the wall, and in an agonized voice
implores God to give her back her dead child. Farther on
two Jews, wearied with praying, are talking business. " Have

you bought ? What have you paid ? Too dear ! " and so on. After this interlude they recommence praying and weeping.

An old Rabbi is sitting in his corner on a stone or an empty wine box with the inevitable " Bordeaux " mark, and with eyes full of tears reads in his book : " O God, the heathen are come into thine inheritance ; the holy temple have they defiled ; they have laid Jerusalem in heaps. . . . We are become a reproach to our neighbours, a scorn and derision to them that are round about us. How long, Lord ? Wilt thou be angry with us for ever ? Shall thy jealousy burn like fire ? "

Fragments of an interesting litany are often sung here :

I.

Reader: Because of the palace which is deserted,
People : We sit alone and weep.
Reader : Because of the Temple which is destroyed,
Because of the walls which are broken down,
Because of our greatness which is departed,
Because of the precious stones of the Temple ground to powder,
Because of our priests who have erred and gone astray,
Because of our kings who have contemned God,
People : We sit alone and weep.

II.

Reader : We beseech Thee, have mercy on Zion.
People: And gather together the children of Jerusalem.
Reader : Make speed, make speed, O Deliverer of Zion.
People : Speak after the heart of Jerusalem.
Reader : Let Zion be girded with beauty and with majesty.
People : Show favour unto Jerusalem.
Reader : Let Zion find again her kings.
People : Comfort those who mourn over Jerusalem.
Reader : Let peace and joy return to Jerusalem.
People : Let the branch of Jerusalem put forth and bud.

(*See also No.* 13, *Smaller Example.*)

95. The Pearl Mosque in Agra.

58 x 78.

The temple is of white marble in Mauresque style, of very fine proportions. There are few or no ornaments, but the beauty of lines and of the material compensate for it. The mosque was built in the year 1654, at the time when the first signs of decay in the Mogul art began to be felt.

(*See Smaller Example, No. 42.*)

96. Dressing the Wounded.

39 x 138

The carts used in transporting the wounded were the same as those in which the supplies of rusks were brought to the army, and these were supplemented by local carts. After the third assault on Plevna the whole road from this town to the Danube was thronged by transport trains of these carts ; what with the primitive construction of the vehicles and the execrable roads, the agonies of the wounded were horrible beyond description, and the most trifling wounds gangrened and became mortal. During a removal from one hospital to another, lasting usually several days, in the heat and dust, all the wounds became full of worms, and the Sisters of Mercy had to display extraordinary fortitude in cleaning, dressing, and healing all this. Whatever the behavior of women in other countries and other armies may be, I know not, but this I can say, that the Russian woman showed herself a true heroine in her devotion, her honor and unselfishness.

97. The Spy.

60 x 50

"Come and see them leading away a spy," said General Skobeleff (father of my friend, Michael Skobeleff), to me.

No. 97.   THE SPY.

We seated ourselves on a bench opposite a house entered by Colonel P. of the staff, and an aide-de-camp of the commander-in-chief, who had just arrived from headquarters. Before the porch were posted soldiers with fixed bayonets, two in front and two on either side. The examination and interrogatories lasted some time, and half an hour must have elapsed before we saw the figure of a tall, dark man on the threshold. He was handsomely dressed, and wore his cap a little on one side. At the sight of the soldiers he turned somewhat paler, stopped, took a deep breath, and thrusting his hands into his pockets began descending the steps without moving his eyes from the soldiers.

98. The Adjutant.

19 X 29

Si jeune et si décoré.

99. The Road of the War Prisoners.

70 X 118

The road from Plevna to the Danube for a distance of thirty to forty miles was literally strewn with the bodies of frozen wounded Turks. The frost set in so suddenly, and with such severity, that the brave defenders of Plevna in their stiff frozen overcoats were too weak to resist it, and by ones and twos fell on the road, and were frozen to death. With the assistance of a Cossack companion I tried to raise some of these fallen and set them on their feet, but they fell down again, so completely enfeebled were they, though evidently anxious to follow their comrades. Sitting and lying in the snow, they moved hands and feet as though they longed to be moving, but were powerless. The next day their movements became less, and they lay on the snow by the hundred, prostrate on their backs, moving lips and fingers as they gradually and slowly froze to death. (Having heard that this kind of death was one of the least painful, I closely examined the faces of the corpses lying in every imaginable position along the road, and convinced myself that every face bore the impress of deep suffering. This form of death, then, is evidently also not painless.) I recollect two Turks in particular—an old man, and quite a youth, seated by the side of the road, warming themselves by a diminutive fire of a few sticks. When I stopped my horse near them in the morning, the youth tried to speak to me, but burst into tears, and I could only understand, " Oh, Effendi, Effendi ! " I answered, pointing to Heaven, " Allah, Allah ! " The older man was silent, and looked gloomily down. On returning to Plevna in the evening I sought out the place where I had left them ; the little fire had long burnt itself out, the young Turk lay prostrate and apparently dead, while his companion sat motionless beside him, bent almost double. He, too, was probably also dead.

The first few days there was nobody to move the dead and dying, so that passing carts and gun-carriages crushed their bodies into the snow and rendered it impossible to extricate them without spoiling the road.

100. A Resting-place of Prisoners.

7· x 117

I remember a party of eight to ten thousand prisoners at Plevna overtaken by a snow-storm. They extended along the high-road for a great distance and sat closely huddled together, with heads bent down, and from all this mass of human beings there rose a dull moaning from thousands of voices as they slowly and in measure repeated, "Allah ! Allah ! Allah ! " The snow covered them, the wind blew through their chilled forms ; no fire, no shelter, no bread. When the word of command to start was given, I saw some of the older, venerable Turks, probably fathers of families, crying like children, and imploring the escort to let them go as far as the town to dry their clothes, warm themselves, and rest ; but this was strictly forbidden, as there were such numbers of them, and only one answer was returned to all their supplications, " Forward, forward ! "

101. The Window of Selim-Shisti's Monument.

105 x 83

The great Mogul Akbar, the most powerful Indian chief, erected this monument over the remains of his friend and counsellor, Selim-Shisti, a man who led a most holy life, and whose memory is still held in reverence by all the Mohammedans of India. This window, like the monument itself, is of pure white marble. On the veranda surrounding it pilgrims converse with the descendants of the saint, who perform religious offices without being themselves in the least degree holy.

102. Skobeleff at Shipka.

70 x 158

The day after the battle at Shipka, where the Turks under Vessel Pasha were surrounded and taken prisoners, Skobeleff reviewed his troops, and thanked them for the victory. The regiments were drawn up facing the Turkish forts, with their left flank on Mount St. Nicholas. Putting spurs to his horse, the general galloped down the line, and, waving his cap, shouted to the men : "In our country's name, on the part of our Sovereign, I thank you, my comrades." It would be difficult to describe the enthusiasm that prevailed as the soldiers threw their caps in the air and cheered repeatedly. Skobeleff was evidently deeply moved, as I saw tears in his eyes. Indeed, all were overjoyed at the success,

No. 102. Skobeleff at Shipka.

every one kept holiday—except the dead, slain but yester-day, and still littering the ground before the trenches.

103. The Turkish Hospital at Plevna.

70 x 158

After the surrender of this town we found the whole of the principal street filled with hospitals ; the houses on both sides were crowded with sick and wounded. In the company of a doctor and another friend, I visited these "hospitals." At the first gateway I met the owner of the house, and learned of him that there were thirty sick men in it, "but some," he added, "must have died." We entered. No words can express the horrors : the fetid air, the filth, the dirt, and in the midst of it all what a scene of death ! nothing but death ! The same thing in the next house, the third, fourth, tenth, twentieth, fiftieth—all alike. Now and again something stirred in a corner under a heap of rags, showing that life was not quite extinct. In one house only a wounded Turk met us, with terribly inflamed eyes. He had heard approaching footsteps, and had probably wanted to meet us, but he was only able to stand by sup-porting himself against the wall, and mutter a few words between his teeth ; he could not articulate. In the panic of the last few days before the surrender of the town, and also afterwards, the Turks forgot and abandoned their sick and wounded ; the Turkish doctors and surgeons all dis-persed, and had to be caught and forcibly made to enter the hospitals. But it was almost a hopeless task, for this mass of brave men were beyond human aid.

104. The Kreml, from the opposite side of the River Moskva. This is one of the most curious sights in existence. I do not know any other city in the world that would pre-sent more original and even more striking views.

No. 104.   THE KREML.

1. The Orujeinaia Palata (Treasury), containing a rare collection of historical treasures.
2. The Great Palace of the Kremlin.
3. The Church of the Conception. This is the private church of former Tsars and Grand Dukes. The Tsarinas attended religious service in its chantry.
4. Terema, or Old Palace of the Tsars.
5. Church of the Archangel. Here are buried the Tsars and Grand Dukes. (In more recent times the Russian Emperors are buried in St. Petersburg.)
6. Church of the Assumption. Here the Metropolitans (as formerly the Patriarchs) of the Russo-Greek Church, are elected and inducted; here, too, the Tsars are crowned, and State ceremonies are solemnized.

7. Tower of Ivan Veliki (John the Great). The largest of its monster bells, named after the Tsar, fell to the ground, where it lay till raised on its present pedestal.
8. Chudof Monastery.
9. Small palace of the Kremlin.
10. Convent. Burial-place of the Tsarinas and Grand Duchesses.
11. Gate of Our Saviour. Every one passing through it must uncover the head.
12. Church of the Blessed St. Basil.
13. Walls of the Kremlin.
14. River Moskva.

750~

105. **Crucifixion by the Romans.**

117 X 157

4000

106. **Blowing from Guns in British India.**

117 X 157

15~

107. **Hanging in Russia.**

117 X 157

} " Eye for Eye, Tooth for Tooth."

108. **The Private Mosque of the Great Moguls in the Palace of Delhi.**

156 X 195

2000

Surrounded from all sides with white marble walls, the mosque is strongly reflected—no dark shadows—fresh, cool, airy. I like the Moslem mosques; the prayer is simple and not less solemn than that of the Christians; but the Deity is not represented there in any painted or sculptured form. You may feel that God is present at your prayer, but where is He ?—it is left to your soul to discover it. . . .

2100

109. **The Forgotten Soldier.***

These lines are by the artist, and are translated from the original by W. R. S. Ralston.

(a) Hushed is the battle : silence fills
Anew the hollows of the hills,
Save where, amid the rocks alone,
Is feebly heard a dying groan.

* * * * * *

Above the topmost snowy height,
A somber spot in azure light,
On steady wing, intent on prey,
A vulture wends its circling way.

(b) Far from its watch-place in the skies,
A gleam of scarlet it espies,
Amid the bushes, where the mist
The forehead of the hill has kissed.

* Only one of these large pictures could be exhibited here.

No. 110. THE FUTURE EMPEROR OF INDIA.

Sweeps the vulture widely round,
Sees what cumbereth the ground,
Folds its pinions ; from afar
Earthward drops—like a falling star.

(c) Together to the banquet fly
Its comrades, summoned by its cry ;
With eager beaks and claws the troop
Of vultures on the booty swoop.

But hark ! fresh pinions cleave the air—
The eagles to the feast repair ;
Above the dead, with hunger's rage,
The rival bands in fight engage.

How long the contest lasted none
Can say, nor which the vict'ry won ;
Only the hills, the battle o'er,
Have seen the vulture wheel no more.

    *   *   *   *   *   *

All in the mountains is at peace,
There all things flourish, gleam, increase ;
Day follows day, the years go by—
The soldier's bones forgotten lie.

110. The Future Emperor of India.

193 x 284

When the Prince of Wales traveled through India the
native chiefs vied with one another in the splendor and
ceremony of their receptions. There might be seen con-
spicuous red costumes by the side of picturesque remnants
of mediæval taste ; above all gleamed costly jewels, gold
and silver. . . . When I came first to Jeypore I found
that the houses were agreeably painted in different colors :
green, blue, yellow ; but on returning to the spot later on, I
was perfectly astonished : previous to the entrance of the
Prince of Wales into his residence, the Maharajah of Jeypore gave strict orders to strew with roses all the buildings
of his town, without exception.

FIRST AFTERNOON SALE.

THURSDAY, NOVEMBER 19TH.

BEGINNING PROMPTLY AT 2:30 O'CLOCK.

— -

EAST INDIAN METAL WORK.

Composed mainly of objects of domestic utility, but containing an interesting series of images used in Brahminical worship.

111 Tall-necked metal vase, with stopper; chiseled ornamentation.

112 Vase, metal, with black enamel richly inlaid with silver and brass.

113 Pitcher, metal, with handle formed of three serpents; chiseled ornamentation.

114 Tray, metal, with black enamel, and brass and silver inlaying.

115 Pitcher, metal, tall neck, with snake for handle.

116 Pitcher, metal, with snake handle and hinged lid.

117 Brass salver, round, with richly chiseled and indented design.

118 Another.

119 Long-necked metal vase, with lid, ornamented in relief.

120 Vase, metal, long neck with top, chiseled ornamentation.

121 Vase, metal, with black enamel, inlaid with silver and brass.

122 Goblet, metal, hammered and chiseled, with lid.

123 Brass tray, round.

124 Pitcher, metal, tall neck, with snake handle.

125 Another.

126 Round tray, metal, with fish in relief chiseling.

127 Dish, metal, with silver inlaying.

128 Bowl, same material and style.

129 Brass statuette of the sacred bull. Brahminical worship.

130 Brass statuette, a praying deity. Brahminical worship.

131 Brass statuette, a dancing deity. Brahminical worship.

132 Brass statuette, a deity in warrior's garb. Brahminical worship.

133 Brass statuette of Vishnu. Brahminical worship.

134 A carved copper spoon.

135 Brass statuette of a dog.

136 Brass statuette of Vishnu. Brahminical worship.

137 Brass statuette of a deity. Brahminical worship.

138 Another.

139 Brass statuette of Vishnu. Brahminical worship.

140 A copper belt buckle, carved.

141 Brass statuette of Vishnu. Brahminical worship.

142 A brass figure, standing, holding a brass tray with compartments for condiments.

143 Brass salt cellar.

144 Ornamental knife rest, copper.

145 Another.

146 A pair of cymbals.

147 Pitcher, metal, incised ornamentation.

148 Jar with top, incised metal.

149 Metal cup with top, polished and engraved.

150 Tray, clover-leaf shape, incised metal.

151 Pitcher, metal, with hinged top.

152 Tray, brass, ornamental incising.

153 Bowl, with cover, incised metal.

154 Tray, metal, four-leaved clover shape, incised ornamentation.

155 Temple bell, carved.

156 Bell, fine carving.

157 Dish, metal, incised ornaments.

158 Bowl with cover, carved metal.

159 Platter and bowl with top, incised metal.   2 pieces.

160 Jar with top, metal, hammered and engraved ornaments.

161 Bowl, metal, with black enamel and ornamentation.

162 Vase, metal, with top.

163 Circular tray, brass, with fine color decoration, from Cashmere.

164 Vase, metal, with lid, chiseled decoration.

165 Cup, enameled metal.

166 Vase, metal, enameled.

167 Vase, metal, large, with engraved ornamentation.

168 Tray, metal, round, chiseled ornaments.

169 Another.

170 Covered box, chiseled metal.

RUSSIAN RELIGIOUS EMBLEMS, ETC.

These objects afford an idea of the quality and progress of devotional art in Russia from the earliest period. Among the more ancient of them are many unique pieces. Through the collection can be traced the Byzantine influence which molded the early art of Russia, and the gradual growth of the national æsthetical idea in an independent and individual direction. The rude ancient crosses and votive medallions are of great interest, and the more modern work shows much originality and skill of execution. The finer and more costly crucifixes and chains were made to be worn as part of the outer attire. The less pretentious were worn under the clothing. The larger crosses and triptychs were used for wall shrines; every orthodox house in Russia, no matter how humble, having its special domestic altar. The specimens range from the very beginning of the art of working metals in Russia to the present century, and show every style of casting, chiseling, carving, and engraving metals there in use.

171 Hermit's belt. A very curious ancient work of wrought iron, formed of alternate chains and crosses, making a ponderous but flexible girdle to confine the robe at the waist.

172 Panel, oblong, of carved wood from the interior of a Russian church. Early work.

173 Carved openwork ornament, wood, from the decorations of a shrine or altar in a Russian church. Seventeenth century.

174 Rosary, with beads and cross in carnelian, well finished and highly polished. Excellent Russian work.

175 Wooden beads of a rosary, without cross. Earliest Russian devotional work.

176 Rosary of knotted cord, divided into sections by bone beads and with a cross of cord. Very curious old work, probably of rural origin.

177 Rosary of leather, with plain leather tabs instead of cross. This form of rosary is common in the districts of Russia remote from the large cities, and with the poor.

178 Another, of white canvas cloth, the tabs of same.

179 Another, leather, same style.

180 Hermit's rosary, of horsehair.

181 Another, leather, with silk tabs, embroidered with gold thread.

182 Another, leather, with the leather tabs bearing religious inscriptions stamped in gold.

183 Rosary, the beads of carved peach and cherry pits, connected by silver chain and with silver mounts. Characteristic Russian work.

184 Another, the beads of wood, silver mount and mother-of-pearl cross.

185 Another, the beads of ivory nuts, colored, carved, and silver mounted, with the cross of mother-of-pearl.

186 String of antique wooden beads, without cross.

187 Rosary, the beads of coral and bone, the cross of pearl, connected by a silver chain.

188 Another, the beads covered with silk and strung on silver wire.

189 Another, the beads of date-stones, with a wooden cross.

190 Another, carved bone beads, cross of carved bone, and silver mount.

191 Another, of Russia leather, the tabs embroidered with beads.

192 Rosary, clouded amber beads with pearl cross.

193 Another, with small sea-shells as beads, and a cross of glass beads.

194 Another, leather, with bead embroidery on tabs.

195 Rosary, the beads of pierced ivory, some white and some stained with color, mounted in gold, and the cross in coral and seed pearls. An elaborate, characteristic, and extremely rare old piece of Russian carving.

196 String of black carved beads.

197 Rosary, the beads of carved cherry-pits, with wooden cross. In certain districts of Russia the cherry- and peach-orchards make these species of rosaries easy of local manufacture.

198 Rosary. The beads are of the stones of some fruit, carved and varnished, and connected by a silver chain. The cross is of wood, holding in a glass-covered cavity a sacred relic.

199 Shrine for wall, of carved wood. The centre panel shows the crucifixion, surrounded by eleven panels representing scenes from the life of Christ. The panels are set off by dividing strips of brass. Seventeenth century.

200 Shrine for wall, of wood carved in architectural forms, and enclosing a painted central panel showing the figure of a saint. The work preserves traces of ancient gilding and color. Sixteenth century.

201 Picture for shrine, showing Christ, painted in oil on a wooden panel, with a metal mount enriched with enameling for a frame. Seventeenth century.

202 Picture for shrine. Christ preaching, painted on a panel and framed in brass with cloisonné enamel. About the same period.

203 Picture for shrine. The Virgin and Child are painted on a panel, over which a frame is made of sheet brass ornamented with a design of dotted ornamental figures. About the same period.

204 Cross of wood, with elaborate under-cutting. This is a very old piece, and preserves traces of having been originally painted. Early sixteenth century.

205 Silver neck-chain, with cross of silver, enameled and gilt.

206 Chain for neck, silver and silver-gilt, with cross of the same style and material.

207 Silver neck-chain, with silver cross in open work. Very old.

208 Neck-chain in silver-gilt and silver-gilt cross set with emeralds, rubies, and sapphires.

209 Silver neck-chain, with old gilding and a silver cross in open-work.

210 Another, with old gilding.

211 Neck-chain of silver, with cloisonné enamel and cross to match.

212 Small chain of silver-gilt, with a gilt cross.

213 Silver chain in old open-work, with circular medallion of tortoise-shell, representing on the face the Virgin and Child, and on the back Christ on the bier.

214 Silver chain and cross. The cross shows the crucifixion in chiseled and hammered metal.

215 Silver chain, with gilt cross enriched with jewels.

216 Silver chain in small links, with a medallion showing a saint praying and an ecclesiastic preaching.

217 Silver chain, with cross with incised figures touched with gilding. The cross is made in sheet-silver and opens to serve as a relic box.

218 Silver chain, gilt ; cross of same.

219 Cross, ornamented in chiseled silver.

220 Another.

221 Another, with enamel.

222 Another, same style.

223 Cross of chiseled silver.

224 Another, with a rude figure of the Saviour and showing traces of gilding.

225 Silver cross, enameled and gilt.

226 Cross, gilded and enameled, with inscriptions on the reverse.

227 The same, without enameling.

228 Another, very old, and worn with use.

229 Another, in silver, gilt.

230 The same, in plain silver and without enamel.

231 Another, in very fine enamel and gilding.

232 Agate cross, mounted with old silver, gilded and set with raw pearls.

233 The same, gilded, enameled, and set off with coral beads.

234 Silver medallion, with cross and inscription incised.

235 Silver cross, with very old enameling.

236 Medallion, with cross, showing old gilding.

237 Circular medallion, with crucifixion in relief.

238 Silver cross, with old enamel.

239 Another.

240 Another.

241 Another.

242 Silver cross, gilt.

243 Another, with ancient enameling.

244 Very ancient silver cross, with letters of inscription in relief.

245 Silver cross, of primitive form.

246 Old silver cross.

247 Silver cross, gilded, with crucifixion on face. Very fine.

248 Old silver cross, open-work ornamentation.

249 Another, with old enameling.

250 Another.

251 Silver cross, flat, with gilding.

252 Cross, of wood, with a silver rim. The carving of the front shows the crucifixion, and of the back the baptism of our Saviour.

253 Cross, old silver.

254 Another, enameled and gilt.

255 Another, flat.

256 Agate cross, silver-gilt mounts with pearls and jewels.

257 Cross of old silver, with colored enamels.

258 Old silver cross.

259 Another, flat.

260 Another, open-work.

261 The same.

262 The same.

263 Another, with ancient enameling.

264 Another.

265 Old silver cross.

266 Medallion in high-repoussé silver, of a saint.

267 Angels' heads in silver (2) to form a relic box.

268 Center panel and one wing of a triptych in chiseled brass.

269 Medallion, brass, with enamel and carved figures.

270 Ancient copper cross.

271 Ancient brass cross, showing the crucifixion, with angels.

272 Triptych, of brass, carved.

273 Wing of brass triptych, divided into four panels, carved and enameled.

274 Brass panel, carved and enameled.

275 Cross, brass, very old.

276 Triptych, brass, relief carving and enamel finish.

277 Brass panel, showing in relief and enamel St. George and the Dragon.

278 Copper cross, dated 1812.

279 Ancient copper cross.

280 Another, with Christ preaching in the center.

281 Square medallion, with saint.

282 Small brass cross.

283 Brass cross, silver-gilt.

284 Another, with enameling.

285 Brass medallion.

286 Double cross, of metal, gilt.

287 Metal cross, elaborately carved and enameled, with finely incised inscription on the back.

288 An old copper cross.

289 Brass cross, with old enamel.

290 Large brass cross, elaborately carved and gilt. The design and execution betray the Byzantine influence very strongly. The Saviour is seen on the cross, with our Lord above his head in a cloud, and a death's-head below his feet.

291 Fragment of a silver-gilt cross.

292 Brass cross, old and elaborately carved.

293 Square medallion, open carving, showing St. George and the dragon. Copper.

294 Square medallion, brass, showing a saint in the act of conferring a benediction.

295 The crucifixion, carved on a stone panel, medallion shape and size.

296 Copper panel, with the Virgin and Child.

297 The same, in brass.

298 Another, with St. George and the dragon.

299 Another, silver.

300 Double cross, old copper.

301 Copper cross, in the form of a winged angel.

302 Brass cross, carved.

303 Brass medallion, with figures of lawgiver and saints.

304 Copper medallion, with Virgin and Child.

305 Very fine copper panel, silver-gilt, showing Christ
with book. The figure is in high relief and admirable in
style and character, and is enclosed in an inscribed border.

306 Panel, silver, or metal silver-gilt, showing the Saviour
seated expounding the law, with kneeling and listening
saints around him. A fine example of the period—early
seventeenth century. Executed with much delicacy and
skill.

307 Large cross, brass, richly gilt and enameled. Our
Saviour is shown, crucified, with Jehovah and angels above,
and a death's-head beneath his feet. An incised text and
description of the divine tragedy is on the reverse of the
cross.

308 The same subject, on a smaller scale, and of earlier
date.

309 Old brass cross.

310 Brass panel, with angel and child.

311 Small diptych, brass, carved and enameled. For
pocket devotions.

312 A triptych in brass.

313 Brass and enameled panel, with three saints.

314 Panel, brass, with head of Christ on a handkerchief.

315 Two parts of a triptych, in brass and enamel.

316 Medallion, showing the figure of a saint with a sword.

317 Cross, brass and enamel.

318 Old brass medallion.

319 Another, with three saints.

320 Another, showing Christ sleeping ; old enamel.

321 Medallion, the Virgin and Child, in brass and enamel.

322 Triptych in brass.

323 Medallion in open carving, showing a saint with a sword.

324 Medallion, brass and enamel, of Virgin and Child.

325 Medallion of brass, showing the entry into Jerusalem. Very delicate and fine.

326 Another, same artist, showing the Annunciation.

327 Old cross, in metal, gilt.

328 Triptych, brass with enamel, with the history of St. John in the center panel.

329 Copper medallion, round, with the figure of Christ as an armed warrior.

330 Another, with rounded top, showing St. John and the Saviour.

331 Brass medallion, showing Christ castigating a sinner.

332 A brass cross.

333 The same, older and smaller.

334 Double, medallion round.

335 Old copper cross.

336 Medallion, brass and enamel, showing the Ascension.

337 A brass cross.

338 A brass medallion.

339 Medallion, brass and enamel, showing the Virgin and Child.

340 An old copper medallion.

341 A brass medallion, with enameling, showing St. George and the Dragon.

342 A brass medallion, showing our Saviour and angels.

343 A round medallion, brass, with the Virgin conferring a blessing.

344 A very old, round copper medallion, showing a saint in the act of blessing.

345 Medallion in brass and enamel.

346 An old cross, copper.

347 Another.

348 Small brass and enamel panel, from a triptych.

349 A cross, brass.

350 Old copper cross.

351 Medallion, the Virgin and Child, copper.

352 Cross, brass, elaborately carved in the Byzantine manner.

353 Triptych in brass and enamel. Illustrating scenes from the life of Christ.

SECOND AFTERNOON SALE.

FRIDAY, NOVEMBER 20TH.

BEGINNING PROMPTLY AT 2:30 O'CLOCK.

RUSSIAN JEWELERS' WORK.

These objects consist almost entirely of ear-rings and of buttons in metal, for male and female attire, and exhibit styles of workmanship and of ornamentation from the earliest period of Russian metal working for ornamental purposes to the present century. They are thoroughly native in character, no attempt having been made to collect the more modern work, in which the fashions of Western Europe prevail.

354 Ear-rings, pair, silver, with topaz in center.

355 Ear-rings, pair, gold, with amethyst.

356 Ear-rings, pair, silver, with rubies.

357 Ear-rings, pair, gold, with basket-shaped pendant, enriched with seed pearls and brilliants.

358 Ear-rings, pair, with amber beads, copper.

359 Ear-rings, pair, silver-gilt, with pearls.

360 Ear-rings, pair, gold, with pear-shaped pendant and raw pearls.

361 Ear-rings, pair, copper, with amethyst and colored stones.

362 Ear-rings, pair, silver enameled, with raw pearls and colored stones.

363 Ear-rings, pair, large, of silver filigree with turquoises; fine specimens.

364 Ear-rings, pair, silver, open-work, with colored stones.

365 Ear-rings, pair, old silver, gilt.

366 Ear-rings, pair, old silver with enamel.

367 Ear-rings, pair, old gold and silver, with brilliants, sapphires, and pearls.

368 Ear-rings, pair, old silver, gilt, with garnets.

369 Ear-rings, pair, old silver, gilt and enameled, with colored stones and pearls.

370 Ear-rings, pair, old gold in open-work, with colored stones and half pearls.

371 Ear-rings, pair, gold, with silver hoops and rubies.

372 Ear-rings, pair, repoussé silver, with pearls, turquoises, and amethysts ; old and fine examples.

373 Ear-rings, pair, gold with seed pearls and brilliants ; very fine in character.

374 Ear-ring (1), copper, silver-gilt, very old and curious.

375 Ear-ring (1), same, but larger in size.

376 Ear-ring (1), old silver, with colored stones.

377 Another.

378 Pendant for necklace, gold, with colored enamels.

379 Brooch, large, 2 clasps, silver, gilt filigree, with long pendants, enriched with topazes and amethysts.

380 Ring for finger, copper, very old.

381 Buttons, silver filigree, pair.

382 Buttons, small, silver, pair.

383 Buttons, silver, gilt, with raw-pearl finish, pair.

384 Buttons, silver filigree, pair.

385 The same.

386 Buttons, silver, gilt, pair.

387 Another pair.

388 Buttons, silver, gilt, pair.

389 Another pair.

390 Buttons, small, silver, gilt, pair.

391 Buttons, old copper and enamel, pair.

392 Buttons, silver filigree, pair.

393 Buttons, silver, gilt, with raw pearls, pair.

394 Buttons, silver open-work, pair.

395 Buttons, large, repoussé silver, pair.

396 Another pair.

397 Large gold button, engraved.

398 Gold button, date-stone shape.

399 Buttons, silver, gilt, globular shape.   5 pieces.

400 Buttons, small, silver, gilt.   5 pieces.

401 Buttons, large, open-work, silver, gilt and enameled.
3 pieces.

402 Buttons, large, silver, gilt.   4 pieces.

403 A button of silver, gilt open-work, conical shape.

404 Buttons, silver, gilt.   4 pieces.

405 A button of old silver, open-work.

406 Buttons, small, silver.   8 pieces.

407 Buttons, gold, enameled and jeweled.   2 pieces.

408 Buttons, silver, gilt and enameled.   2 pieces.

409 Buttons, silver, gilt.   2 pieces.

410 Buttons, small, silver, enameled.   2 pieces.

411 Four buttons.

412 Two buttons.

413 Two buttons.

414 Buttons, silver.   2 pieces.

415 Three buttons.

416 Buttons, silver, gilt and enameled.   3 pieces.

MISCELLANEOUS CURIOS.

These are mainly objects gathered by Mr. Verestchagin during his travels in the Orient, and are of great historical, artistic, and ethnological interest.

417 Statue of Vishnu, in white marble.   Hindustan.

418 Statuette of the sacred bull, in slate.   Hindustan.

419 Another, larger, in the same style.

420 Statuette of Vishnu, in soapstone.   Hindustan.

421 Small statuette of Vishnu, in black basalt, very old and curious Hindustani carving.

422 Statuette of Vishnu, carved in slate.   Hindustan.

423 A large brass brooch.   Indian.

424 A brass disk with pendants.

425 A Buddhistic temple drum, double.

426 A Buddhistic priest's head-dress, with painted deities and gilding.

427 A double temple drum, formed of the upper portions of human skulls. From Thibet.

428 Another.

429 A painted clay figure of a woman holding a dog, representing the Hindu idea of an Englishwoman.

430 A knife case, with knife and purse, in silk.

431 A double pouch or purse, silk.

432 Silk tabs for a sash.

433 A single pouch or purse, embroidered.

434 A knife, in a shagreen case, with a leather pouch.

435 A silk bag.

436 A knife and chopsticks, in a wooden case with ornaments in brass and silver. Part of an Indian gentleman's traveling outfit.

437 A double case, silk embroidered, containing Hindu papers.

438 Three rice-bowls, of wood.

439 A human thigh-bone, used for a musical pipe. From Thibet.

440 Another.

441 Another.

442 Vase, with top and tray, of inlaid wood. Indian work. 2 pieces.

443 Pouch, of leather, for flint and steel.

444 Knife and chopsticks, in case with gold mounting.

445 A serpent. Hindu manufacture.

446 A pouch, leather.

447 A Thibetan prayer-wheel.

448 Another.

449 Wine bowl, made of the top part of a human skull. From Thibet.

450 Painted clay statuette of Vishnu. Hindu workmanship.

451 The vertebræ of a serpent, strung as beads.

452 A leather pouch.

453 Another.

454 A silk sash. Hindu.

455 Wooden dish, finely decorated in colors. From Cashmere.

456 Bracelets and anklets of ivory. Hindu. 3 pieces.

457 Bracelet, gilt. Hindu.

458 Bracelets and anklets. Hindu. 17 pieces.

459 Bone beads. From Thibet.

460 Bone beads. From Thibet.

461 Ornamental pendant, for the caparison of a horse.

462 A leather drum.

463 Small clay lamp, from a sepulcher in Palestine.

464 Root of an ancient cypress, from a quarry under the old temple of Jerusalem. 2 pieces.

465 Bead ornament. Hindu.

466 Steel anklet, with flexible links. Hindu.

467 Medallions, silver and enamel. 2 pieces.

468 Armlet of brass beads. Hindu. Necklace, silk and wire. Hindu.

469 Link armlet, silver. Hindu.

470 Child's bracelet, with links, silver. Hindu.

471 Armlet, copper and enamel, old Hindu work.

472 Silver buttons (2). Hindu.

473 Bead bracelet. Hindu.

474 Metal armlet. Hindu.

475 Beads, silver and coral. Hindu.

476 Bracelet, metal. Hindu.

477 Another.

478 Thumb ring, silver. Hindu.

479 Buttons, carved silver, old Hindu workmanship.
5 pieces.

480 Thigh ring, for dancing girl, silver. Hindustan.

481 Ear-ring, with raw stones, old Hindu work. 1 piece.

482 Pendant, glass jewels. Hindu.

483 Another, star shape.

484 Silver pendant, very elaborate and fine. Hindu.

485 Bracelet, chiseled silver. Hindu.

486 Bracelet, gold wire, with center piece, jeweled. Hindu.

487 Pair of clasps, silver and stones. Hindu.

488 Clasps, same work, odd pieces (2).

489 Brooch. Gold and lapis lazuli. Hindu.

490 Necklace of colored stones, with amulet boxes in fine silver work and bead pendant. Hindustan.

491 Ring. Hindu.

492 Another, with double top, silver. Hindu.

493 Silver ring, primitive serpent pattern. Hindu.

494 Another.

495 Necklace, imitation pearls and jewels with pendant. Hindu.

496 Relic box, copper, with effigy of deity. Thibet.

497 Another, of silver.

498 Brooch, serving as relic box, gold and lapis lazuli.

499 Silver pendants. Hindu.

500 Metal beads. Hindu.

501 Silver button or clasp. Hindu.

502 Bead bracelet. Hindu.

503 Silver armlet. Hindu.

504 Relic box, silver. Hindu.

505 Bead bracelet. Hindu.

506 Another.

507 Bead necklace for child.

508 Box for relic, copper and enamel.

509 Relic box, gilt metal and lapis lazuli.

510 Silver pendant, very elaborate and fine. Hindu.

511 Amulet in metal.

512 Amulet in cloth.

513 Tiger's claws.   6 pieces

514 Amulet box, gilt metal and lapis lazuli.

515 Silver ornament. Hindu.

516 Pendant, silver and enamel. Hindu.

517 Bead ornament. Hindu.

518 Bead bracelet.   Hindu

519 Silver anklet.   Hindu.

520 Metal bracelet.   Hindu.

521 Beads.   Hindu.

522 Bead bracelet.   Hindu.

523 Hindu ornament.

524 Thibetan art, a series of 7 drawings.

525 Skull of a small animal.

526 Sacred Buddhistic tablet, with carved figure on slate.

527 Another, of sandstone.

528 Another, of sandstone.

529 Stone fragment with inscription.   Thibetan.

530 Another.

531 Another.

532 Stone, in natural state, with inscription, from Thibet.

533 Another.

534 Beads of dried fruit, 4 strings.   Thibetan.

535 Reproductions of church carvings, 36 pieces, gilt. Russian.

536 Marbles from the Mosque of Omar.   6 pieces.

537 Glazed tiles from the old Duma, or council house, of Moscow, from Wologda, Kostroma, etc.   10 pieces.

538 Oriental glazed tiles.   9 pieces.

539 Tiles from the Mosque of Shah Zinda at Samarkand ; framed in plush.   3 pieces.

540 Glazed tiles from Jerusalem, the Mosque of Omar, and various other buildings ; framed.   2 pieces.

541 Others, framed.   2 pieces.

542 Others, framed.   2 pieces.

543 Others, framed.   2 pieces.

544 Others, framed.   2 pieces.

545 Others, framed.   3 pieces.

546 Others, framed.   2 pieces.

547 Turquoise glaze tile, from the Mosque of Shah Zinda at Samarkand. Framed in plush.

548 A piece of marble trellis-work from the tomb of Tamerlane in the Mosque of Ghur-Amir. Framed in plush.

549 A fragment of marble from the tomb of Tamerlane's son in the Mosque of Ghur-Amir. Framed in plush.

550 Tiles. Framed in plush.   2 pieces.

551 Hanging pictures, devotional subjects, 4 panels, from Thibet.

552 Mask of Thibetan deity.

553 Death's-head mask of Thibetan deity.

554 Deer's head, from Thibet.

555 Mask of Thibetan deity.

556 Mask of Thibetan deity crowned with skulls.

557 A Himalayan eagle, stuffed.

558 Cloth bag or purse, with Russian and Oriental coins in gold, silver, and copper.   93 pieces.

PHOTOGRAPHY.

559. An Ambush.

A small Russian detachment, sent on a reconnoitring expedition, has encamped in a valley, unaware that the enemy

(Uzbeks and Kirghizes) is concealed in the neighboring hills, watching a favorable moment for the attack.

560. The Surprise.

No sooner has the detachment dispersed, intent on various errands, than masses of the enemy are upon it, uttering terrible cries, and brandishing their swords and spears. All those Russians who had gone a little distance are cut down ; the remainder assemble and prepare to sell their lives dearly. (I was present at one of these engagements.)

561. Surrounded—Pursued.

The handful of brave survivors, surrounded on all sides, retreat fighting. They have beaten off the enemy, and keep him at a respectful distance with their rifle fire. The dead are abandoned, the wounded led away. An officer is carried by his men. (A picture, representing the total destruction of a detachment in a mountain defile, where the last survivors are shot down and killed by fragments of rock hurled from the crags above, was not finished.)

562. Presenting the Trophies.

In the palace of the Emir of Bokhara, at Samarkand. In the background is the celebrated " Kok-tash "—the throne of Tamerlane. The heads of the slaughtered Russians are brought to the Emir, who rewards the bearers of these trophies with the customary robes of honor, each individual receiving according to the number of heads he brings.

563. Triumph.

The Emir presents his people with the heads of their foes. These are then stuck upon high poles in the principal square in Samarkand, in front of the mosques. A mollah preaches on the text : " Thus God ordains that infidels should perish ; there is only one God ! "

564. Returning Thanks for the Victory.

The Emir and his retinue offer up thanksgivings for the victory at the grave of Tamerlane—great Mohammedan saint of our day—noted conqueror and robber of former times.

565. Apotheosis of War.

Dedicated to all the great conquerors, past, present, and future. This picture is not the creation of the artist's imagination—it is historically correct. Tamerlane and many other heroes raised such monuments on their battle-fields, leaving the bones to be cleansed and whitened by the sun and rain, by wolves, jackals, and birds of prey. Not very long ago, about 1860, the celebrated German scientist, Schlagintweit (while in the English service), was murdered by Valikhan-tiure, despot of Jetyshar in Kashgaria, and his head was thrown on a similar, though smaller pyramid, which it was the Kahn's amusement to watch growing daily bigger.

566. Gate of Tamerlane.

In the palace at Samarkand.

567. Gate of a Mosque.

Two friars of the begging order of Nakshbendi engaged in the usual way ; a common mode of passing spare time in Central Asia.

568. Hush ! Let them Enter.

During the defence of Samarkand by the Russians, an assault was momentarily expected through one of the breaches made by the enemy in the walls. The shouts of the approaching multitude were audible, and I begged Colonel N., then in command of the garrison, to sally out to meet them, but his answer was, " Hush ! let them enter."

.

569. They have entered.

The assault has been repulsed, and the tired soldiers are calmly smoking their pipes, whilst a few remove the dead bodies.

570. From Mountain to Valley.

In autumn the Kirghiz abandon their encampments near the snow line, and remove to winter quarters. In order not to damage their clothes by packing them into boxes, they attire themselves in all their best robes, so that one of these migrations has all the appearance of a holiday procession.

571. Underground Prison at Samarkand.

Built of brick, with a narrow funnel-shaped mouth, the only means of ingress and egress being by a rope with loops. When I descended into this gloomy dungeon I almost fainted from the stench and foul air, and could with difficulty make my sketch. And here prisoners remained for more than ten years in succession without ever breathing pure air. This infernal den was called the bug-hole, and I believe a certain kind of bug or other insect was purposely bred to stock it, and prey day and night upon the unfortunate victims. Let me add, however, that I found no bugs in it.

In this very dungeon the ill-fated Stoddart and Conolly were imprisoned for a time. At the instance of the Russian agent they were released, and might have availed themselves of their opportunity to escape, but refused to do so (an historical fact).

572. The Mortally Wounded Soldier.

The first man I saw wounded was a soldier who had been struck by a bullet in the chest. He threw away his gun, placed both hands over his wound, and began reeling like a drunken man. "Oh, comrades, they have killed me, they have killed me. My death has come to me." . . . "Lie down, brother," answer his companions, but he continues to stagger a little longer, then falls prone to the ground.

573. The Kirghiz Sportsman.

The favorite pastime of the rich Kirghiz is hawking. For this purpose hawks and eagles are trained by being blindfolded, and by never being allowed to sleep.

574. Sale of a Slave.

575. Central Asian Politicians.

Ragged, half drunk with opium, they are nevertheless among the keenest of politicians. They know and discuss not only what the Ak Padishah—i.e., White Tsar—does and says, but what he thinks and is meditating.

576. Beggars at Samarkand.

Along the highways leading to the chief places of resort they may be seen by the dozen, sometimes sitting on the ground, and importunately begging alms.

578. Chorus of Dervishes or Divans.

Of the aforesaid monastic order of Nakshbendi. They parade the streets in troops led by their chief singer, and howl unceasingly until they receive alms. Every novice, on joining the fraternity, receives a cap, a belt, a bowl made of a gourd, and a dress of variegated patches of stuff obtained by begging at the bazaar.

579. Dividing the Spoil.

580. The Conquerors.

Turks stripping the Russian dead on the field of Telisch.

581. Parleying.

" Surrender ! " " Go to the devil ! "

582. The Forgotten Soldier.

In Turkestan. (The original picture was destroyed by the artist.)

583. Russian Graves on the Shipka.

THIRD AFTERNOON SALE.

— — ———— ·

RUSSIAN APPLIED ART FOR HOUSE-HOLD USE.

These objects were assembled by Mr. Verestchagin for use in his artistic studies of his native land. Among them will be found many of extremely curious antiquity and great rarity. Some furnish the origin of forms of utensils still in common use, while others have been entirely superseded by more modern and convenient contrivances. Together they constitute a little museum of Russian household appliances, from the earliest period of their adaptation by human ingenuity to domestic utility.

584 A wooden ladle, of primitive style. The handle is terminated by a rude carving representing a cock. Very early period, rural workmanship.

585 Table knives (2), varying in shape of blade. The handles are of curious form, and elaborately ornamented with cloisonné enamel, on a brass foundation. Eighteenth century.

586 Cup called "Koobky," of the time of Peter the Great. It is formed of a globular cocoanut shell, mounted with silver, with silver foot and lid, plain in finish. The

color and surface of cut and mounting betray its age and long use.

587 Cup called "Koobky," of the time of Peter the Great. It has a cocoanut-shell bowl of oval shape, and lid, mounted in ornamented silver. The handle of the lid is formed by the Russian eagle, of chiseled silver, and the cup is of graceful form and proportions.

588 A cup for vodka. Metal. Quite elaborately carved and enameled, with a foot. Seventeenth century.

589 Vodka cup of beaten silver, engraved in a simple and primitive design. Russian work of the early sixteenth century.

590 A metal scoop for wine, of the XVIIIth century, with the inscription : "Apostle Paul says, 'It is not the wine that is cursed, but cursed is drunkenness.'" The inscription is engraved and the scoop is enriched with ornamental carving.

591 Scoop, of copper, enriched with incised ornamentation. Eighteenth century.

592 Beetle or thumper, used for cleansing clothes in washing. Of hard wood, carved in primitive Russian style on the upper surface.

593 The same. Larger in size. Both of these pieces show signs of long use. In rural Russia the Oriental practice of beating or pounding the dirt out of linen is still followed, instead of the modern process of scrubbing on a board or beating by a mangle.

594 Inkstand for desk or table, of brass, with cloisonné enamel in blue, green, and white. Opening for one inkpot. Eighteenth century.

595 Small table or desk inkstand, brass, with cloisonné enamel. Two wells ; same period.

596 Inkstand for table use, brass, with engraved ornament in relief and colors. Two wells ; same period.

597 Old brass inkpot, engraved. Made to be carried about suspended from a button on the coat. Early eighteenth century.

598 The same, with the Russian eagle carved in relief, also for the use of traveling scribes. Same period.

599 The same, with a relief carving, showing on both sides a combat between a tiger and a horse. Excellent example of old Russian chiseling in metal.

600 Ivory casket, carved, painted and gilt. Early eighteenth century.

601 Another, somewhat smaller, and of a different style of decoration, but of the same period.

602 Another, still smaller, and different in style, but of the same period.

603 Iron ornamented box or small coffer.

604 Nut-cracker, of brass, elaborately engraved. Russian eighteenth century work.

605 Candle snuffers, brass, with enamel in colors. Very curious and unusual in shape. Late seventeenth century.

606 Candle snuffers. Iron, with inlaid ornamentation in brass. Conventional shape of the last century.

607 Salt box, of carved wood, in the form of a throne chair, with the seat lifting as a lid.

608 Small open-work casket in silver filigree, of very delicate design and execution. Eighteenth century.

609 Another, different in shape and design, but similar in finish. Eighteenth century.

610 Brass seal, elaborately engraved, in the form of a cylinder, with a screw top, and hollow interior to hold sealing wax. Eighteenth century.

611 Copper bowl, with strong repoussé ornamentation. Early Russian metal work. Seventeenth century.

612 Jewel or money box, of oak, finished on the exterior with ornamental open-work in iron ; antique.

613 Box or casket, of wood, to hold money or jewels. Carved and painted in primitive ornamentation. Very old Russian work.

614 Another, same style and period, with hinged lid.

615 Another, with sliding lid. Earlier period.

616 Another, sliding lid, with carvings of ornaments, animals, etc.

617 Another, smaller, square, with hinged lid.

618 Another, showing on a ground ornamented in relief, rich, ancient gilding.

619 Box or casket to contain valuables. The body is of wood, with an iron open-work exterior finish, and two interior compartments. Seventeenth century.

620 Another, of the same style and period.

621 Another, smaller in size, same origin and time.

622 Another, same origin and time.

623 Candlestick, brass, the stem ornamented by the Russian eagle in open carving, supporting the sconce. Eighteenth century.

624 Iron balls studded with knobs, to be fastened to a strap slung to the wrist and used like a slung-shot, as a weapon. Eighteenth century.

625 A tall brass cup, with a brass tray. The cup is elaborately engraved and further enriched with ornamentation in repoussé. This is a bowl or cup of the kind called "bratina," used for drinking wine, and belonging to the XVIth century, with an inscription in Old Slavo Russian, very difficult to decipher : "And wine will cheat the spells (dispel the charms) the leisure of the toper"—Further on the inscription is not decipherable.

626 Cylindrical basket, made of birch-bark, carved in open-work and showing panels of gaily colored mica in the openings.

627 Another, smaller, same style of workmanship. These baskets illustrate one form of Russian rural workmanship still in common practice.

628 Small box, wood, encased in birch-bark, which is painted. Old Russian.

629 Another, strapped and mounted with iron. Old Russian.

630 Another, same style but smaller in size. These boxes were made to hold seals, small jewels and precious unguents and scents, and perhaps religious relics, and to be carried in the pocket.

RUSSIAN DRESS FABRICS, ETC.

This series includes a number of the richly adorned head-dresses worn by Russian women on gala occasions—veils, kerchiefs and other adjuncts of feminine attire. The laces are in thread, silk, gold and silver wire, and galloons, and among them are many pieces of fine hand-made lace, and embroidery in linen and colored silk, taken from towels, bed-spreads, and other sources. The specimens of Russian art in this line are very characteristic and interesting.

631 Woman's head-dress.

632 Another.

633 Another.

634 Another.

635 Lace.   2 pieces.

636 Silk.   1 piece.

637 Lace.   1 piece.

638 Veil, for head-dress, with flower embroidery.

639 Kerchief.

640 Another.

641 Head-dress for woman.

642 Bead-work head-dress.

643 Another.

644 Cloth.   2 pieces.

645 Bead-worked head-dress.

646 Another.

647 Head-dress.

648 Metal lace.   6 pieces.

649 Head-dress.

650 Another.

651 Gold embroidery.   1 piece.

652 Gold embroidery.   3 pieces.

653 Bead embroidery.

654 Piece of embroidered linen.

655 Lace embroidery.   2 pieces.

656 The same.   1 piece.

657 Piece of embroidered linen.

658 Silver and gold wire embroidery on silk, representing an angel.

659 Lace with silk embroidery.

660 Piece of lace embroidery.

661 Towel, with lace borders.

662 White lace, large piece.

663 Another.

664 Lace with silk insertion.   3 pieces.

665 Wire lace.   5 pieces.

666 Lace embroidery.   1 strip.

667 Silk, with embroidery in silver.

668 Head-dress.

669 Another.

670 Lace, black, green, etc.   4 pieces.

671 Linen lace.   1 piece.

672 Another.

673 Fine white thread lace.   1 piece.

674 Towel, with embroidered ends.

675 Linen embroidery.   1 strip.

676 Piece of lace with appliqué figures.

677 Lace.   1 strip.

678 Another with colored silk work.

679 Wire lace.   3 pieces.

680 Strip, embroidered at ends.

681 Embroidered squares.   2 pieces.

682 Silk embroidery in colors.   2 pieces.

683 Lace.   1 piece.

684 Head-dress.

685 Another.

686 Large head-dress.

687 Lace, silk insertion.

688 Head-dress, with rich bead embroidery.

689 Another.

690 Piece of embroidery.

691 Bead-work on band or sash.

692 Another piece.

693 Bead ornament.

694 Another.

695 Veil for head-dress.

696 Kerchief.

697 Another.

698 Long scarf of linen, with embroidered lace ends.

699 Large strip of white lace, with Russian eagle design.

700 Another, with designs of figures, trees, and temples.

701 Long linen scarf, with embroidered lace ends.

702 Piece of lace embroidery.

703 Piece of white thread lace.

704 Bead and embroidery ornament for dress.

705 Lace, embroidered in silk.

706 Lace, with silk insertion.

707 Lace with colored silk embroidery.

708 Open-work lace square.

709 Another, with embroidery in colored silk.

710 Part of head-dress.

711 Piece of lace.

712 Lace piece, with a peacock in colors.

713 Lace square, with an eagle.

714 Lace piece, with a peacock in colors.

715 Ivory fan, pierced.

716 Fabrics for dress.   16 pieces.

ARMS, ARMOR, ETC.

This department of Mr. Verestchagin's collection is rich chiefly in Oriental weapons and accoutrements of warfare, most of them being of ancient and frequently of historical origin. They constitute a very complete museum of Indian and Central Asian arms and defensive habiliments. The objects nearest our own time are the relics of the last Russo-Turkish war, secured by the artist during his period of alternate service as a soldier and study as an artist on General Skobeleff's staff. Gathered by him as typical objects for use in his pictures, the collection is naturally characterized by artistic beauty and quality. Some of the finest art of the Oriental armorer finds illustration among its numbers, and any one familiar with his paintings will readily recognize in them the good use which he has made of his military museum.

717 Hauberk. East-Indian chain-mail.

718 Another.

719 Armor-belt, iron plates on chain-mail.

720 Helmet, steel, richly inlaid, with chain hood to protect the neck.

721 Helmet, steel, with padded cloth hood.

722 Cavalry sword, with bayonet scabbard attached. Russian.

723 Short sword or cutlass, double-edged, with brass hilt. Russian.

724 Buckler, leather, with copper bosses.

725 Curved sword.

726 Another.

727 Center of shield, steel, with brass ornamentation.

728 Shield, copper center, with iron rim studded with brass bosses and crescents.

729 Sword.

730 Another.

731 Officer's sword, with steel scabbard. Russian.

732 Steel helmet.

733 Complete suit of mail. The hauberk and leggings are of chain-mail, the helmet of steel, with chain hood and face-veil. The arm-pieces are of steel, richly inlaid, with padded cloth hand-guards, and the belt is of inlaid steel in four panels. Very fine. East-Indian work.

734 Sword, curved, with a concave cutting edge.

735 Sword, straight blade.

736 Sword, concave edge.

737 Another.

738 Leaf-shaped stabbing-knife with sweeping hand-grip.

739 Steel mace.

740 Axe.

741 Sword.

742 Another.

743 Long sword, with steel hilt.

744 Steel helmet, with gold inlays, three gold plumes, and chain-mail hood or neck-guard.

745 Another, with one plume.

746 Buckler, with copper bosses.

747 Broad-bladed, curved sword.

748 Another.

749 Shield, steel, with inlays.

750 Curved sword.

751 Another.

752 Shield, steel, engraved.

753 Curved sword.

754 Another.

755 Small shield, steel, gilt, and richly ornamented.

756 Concave-bladed knife, with sheath.

757 Another.

758 Steel helmet, with chain-mail hood and three pompons, engraved.

759 Long gun. Afghan.

760 Long gun, with silver-banded barrel and inlaid and padded stock.

761 Leaf-bladed knife or left-hand dagger.

762 Lance and hook, steel.

763 Another.

764 Buckler of woven rattan, painted.

765 Another.

766 Lance-headed stabbing-knife.

767 Small axe.

768 Another.

769 Pistol, flint-lock, richly mounted in gold and silver ornamentation.

770 Pistol, flint-lock, long barrel.

771 Pistol, flint-lock, sumptuous gold mounting.

772 Another, metal mountings on stock.

773 Trophy of primitive arms from Central Asia.

774 Flint-lock gun.

775 Another.

776 Breech-loading musket, with bayonet. Russian. The stock is sprung as if the weapon had been clubbed in battle.

777 Breech-loading musket. Turkish.

777a Flint-lock gun. Indian.

778 Rifle. Old Indian.

779 Another, with inlayings at breech and stock.

780 Another, very massive barrel and elaborately ornamented stock.

781 Rifle, with bayonet. Turkish.

782 Another. Russian.

783 Another. Russian.

784 Buckler, black leather, with metal bosses.

785 Sword, with grooved blade.

786 Another, with straight blade and rounded point.

787 Small steel shield, engraved with bosses.

788 Steel spear-heads, on horn handles (2).

789 White buckler, bound with iron.

790 Straight-bladed sword, with brass gauntlet guard for hilt.

791 Curved sword.

792 Another.

793 Leather buckler, natural color, with bosses.

794 Straight-bladed sword.

795 Curved sword.

796 Another.

797 Leather buckler with bosses.

798 Sword.

799 Another.

800 Leather buckler, with ornamental center and rim.

801 Straight-bladed sword, with steel gauntlet guard for hilt.

802 Curved sword.

803 Another.

804 Buckler, with four-leafed-clover shape ornament.

805 Sword.

806 Another.

807 Buckler, leather, with brass bosses.

808 Sword, with straight blade.

809 Another.

810 Buckler, with three bosses.

811 Curved sword.

812 Another.

813 Black buckler, with brass bosses.

814 Curved sword.

815 Another.

816 Straight-bladed sword.

817 Buckler, with bosses.

818 Curved sword.

819 Another.

820 Buckler with bosses.

821 Curved sword.

822 Another.

RARE CARPETS, RUGS, TAPESTRIES, ETC.

823 Black bearskin rug.   6 feet x 6 feet.

824 Bengal tiger rug.   10 feet 4 x 7 feet 2 inches.

825 A prayer rug in rich gold embroidery.   32 x 50 inches.

826 A gold-embroidered hanging, garnet velvet field and green velvet border. $52\frac{1}{2}$ x 47 x 63 inches.

827 Rug from Thibet.   66 x 32 inches.

828 Large rug, Agra.   83 x 55 inches.

829 Samarkand rug.   90 x 43 inches.

830 Turkish rug, old Ghiordes.   58 x 37 inches.

831 Rug, Samarkand.   51 x 33 inches.

832 Rug, made in jail of Hydrabad, Scind.   74 x 37 inches.

833 Rug, made in jail of Hydrabad, Scind. 74 x 42 inches.

834 Another. 61 x 35 inches.

835 Another. 63 x 40 inches.

836 Large carpet made in Agra. 18 feet 6 x 12 feet 2 inches.

837 Large carpet, Agra. 17 feet 9 x 12 feet 2 inches.

838 Large Agra carpet. 18 feet 6 x 14 feet.

839 Large Agra carpet, from India. 17 feet 6 x 12 feet.

840 Agra rug. 17 feet 3 x 13 feet 5 inches.

841 Oblong carpet, Agra. 146 x 72 inches.

842 Large Durrie cotton carpet, from India. 20 feet 6 x 24 feet 3 inches.

843 Another. 20 feet 6 x 24 feet 3 inches.

844 Another. 23 feet 6 x 21 feet.

845 Samarkand rug. 45 x 83 inches.

846 Bokarah rug. 48 x 92 inches.

847 Samarkand rug. 69 x 144 inches.

848 Khorassan rug, Persian. 42 x 92 inches.

849 Khorassan rug, Persian. 60 x 132 inches.

850 Khorassan rug, Persian. 70 x 162 inches.

851 Khorassan rug, Persian. 72 x 164 inches.

852 Samarkand rug. 46 x 86 inches.

853 Khorassan rug. 60 x 118 inches.

854 Khorassan rug. 75 x 144 inches.

855 Cashmere rug, made in the Valley of Cashmere. 78 x 128 inches.

856 Samarkand rug. 66 x 168 inches.

857 Samarkand rug. 46 x 92 inches.

858 Agra rug. 20 x 38 inches.

859 Very large carpet, red center, from India, of unusual dimensions, and rare in quality and design. 29 feet 4 x 23 feet. This and the following carpet were made by prisoners in the jail at Agra, from designs copied from various antique rugs in the possession of M. Verestchagin. Such specimens cannot now be duplicated.

860 Another very large carpet, white center, from India, same fine quality as above, and similar in design. 29 feet 4 x 23 feet.

THE AMERICAN ART ASSOCIATION,

MANAGERS.

First and Second Appendix to this Catalogue,

PROGRESS IN ART

AND

REALISM.

——ALSO——

VERESTCHAGIN,

Painter, Soldier, Traveler.

Revised Edition, with much new matter added.

BY

VASSILI VERESTCHAGIN.

TRANSLATED BY

F. H. PETERS, M.A.

Illustrated with many original sketches by the Author.

For sale at the American Art Galleries, and by Booksellers.

www.ingramcontent.com/pod-product-compliance
Lightning Source LLC
Chambersburg PA
CBHW030538270326
41927CB00008B/1427

9783744650991